EXPOSITION

OF THE

PECULIARITIES, DIFFICULTIES AND TENDENCIES

OF

OBERLIN PERFECTIONISM.

PREPARED BY

A COMMITTEE OF THE PRESBYTERY

OF CLEVELAND;

And by the Presbytery ordered to be published under the direction of said
Committee, October 8th, 1840.

CLEVELAND:
PRINTED BY T. H. SMEAD.
....
1841.

THE PERNICIOUS TENDENCY OF ERROR, BY WHOMSOEVER HELD
OR ADVOCATED, AND OUR DUTY IN RELATION TO IT.

SANCTIFICATION is that work of Divine grace by which we
are renewed after the moral image of God, consisting in righteousness and true holiness, set apart for his service, and "made
meet to be partakers of the inheritance of the saints in light."
God's chosen instrument in the work of sanctification, is *his
truth.* '*Sanctify them through thy truth,*' was our blessed Saviour's prayer for all the members of his Church to the end of
time.

Error, on the contrary, has no tendency to make men better.
Opposed, as it is, to truth—to the reality of things—it possesses
no adaptation for "doctrine, for reproof, for correction, for instruction in righteousness." It is fitted only to darken, to pol-
lute and degrade. Though robed in Scripture phrase and boast-
ful of its purifying tendencies, it is found, sooner or later, to
be, by an unalterable law of the moral constitution ruinous in
its results.

It is not, then, in the embrace of error, but "in obeying the
truth through the Spirit," that God's people "purify their souls,"
"growing in grace and in the knowledge of the Lord Jesus
Christ." Hence we are under a most solemn obligation, to dis-
discriminate between truth and error, holding fast to the one,
and carefully rejecting the other. Nor is this duty the less im-
perative, because a system of doctrines, soliciting adoption in
the Church, comes forth bearing the imposing motto of *perfection in holiness;* or because its authors are celebrated for their
piety, and professedly aim at raising the standard of spiritual
attainment among Christians. Names are not always things—
as we have often seen in the past developments of Perfectionism;
nor do even pious men, seeking good ends, always select the
most appropriate means to accomplish those ends. Still less are
the high pretensions of professed reformers, always realized.
It has ever, indeed, been a characteristic of avowed innovators
in Theology, seeking to "make all things new," to begin with
misrepresenting, or caricaturing doctrines that are commonly
received; and then to set forth their own dogmas as the heaven-
appointed remedy, at last discovered, for all existing evils. Pelagianism was not the less false, nor the less pernicious as a
system, because its two authors, Pelagius and Cœlestius "were
universally esteemed," as Mosheim says, "for their extraordinary piety and virtue." Nor was it, at all, the safer to receive

that unscriptural system, instead of God's truth, because they, with so much denunciation of the prevailing doctrines as "tending to lull mankind in a presumptuous and fatal security," began to propagate their novel sentiments, "with no other object in view" than that of "*promoting the progress of holiness and virtue*." The errors and fooleries of Quietism—were they the less opposed to sober truth, and to genuine growth in grace, because sustained, for a season, by the eloquent apologies of the pious Fenelon? And Unitarianism, too—is it any the less fraught with the elements of spiritual death, because its "superior moral tendencies" have been so often and so confidently vaunted by Dr. Priestley, Dr. Channing, and others—tendencies which have never, in real life, been illustrated by any corresponding results?

As if to teach us the folly of looking to any mere man as an infallible guide, in the things of religion, it has been permitted, that currency should be given, sometimes, to dangerous error in doctrine and practice, by the authority, or the sanction of good men. "*To the law, then, and to the testimony.*" And here we we would say, that a system is not to be deemed harmless, even if its peculiar errors should be held, in connection with much precious truth. Nine out of ten propositions, in a system, may be in themselves true, and yet the tenth which is false, be made to sustain to them such a relation as shall give to the system, as a whole, the effect of falsehood. The truth may be so employed, as to give an aspect of harmlessness to the error with which it is associated; and while it may be so *subordinated* in the system, as to have little or no effect to neutralize its bad influence, the truth, thus intermingled, may prevent suspicion of lurking evil, and be the occasion of leading some to embrace that which is unscriptural and false. And then, too, a very common practice of professed reformers is, after caricaturing and misrepresenting the prevailing system of doctrines—to class among their own late, marvellous discoveries, many things which actually belong to the settled Theology of the day, clothed in an unfamiliar garb. These things, which perhaps none deny, they, with an air of triumph, establish by arguments incontrovertible, taking care, meanwhile, to foist in, as plausibly as they can, here and there, the real peculiarities of their system. And thus, having proved so many things, they seem, on the whole, to have greatly the advantage over their assumed opponents, and put forth their scheme of doctrines as something strong in the truth, and new under the sun.

Still less ought a system to be considered as from Heaven, because some or all of its principles can be "*expressed in the language of the Bible.*" If the connection and the laws of sound interpretation be disregarded, passages and phrases *can* be drawn from the Bible, which will express what the Holy Ghost never taught. Hence it has been boasted of Universalism, Unitarianism, and other grossly *unscriptural* systems, that their principles "could be stated in the *very language of inspiration !*"

From the foregoing remarks, it is evident, that the Church of Christ are solemnly bound, by their relation to Him who "is the *Truth,*" as well as "the *way,* and the *life,*" to inquire, previous to the adoption of any new system of doctrines, not merely: Who are its authors?—what do *they* aim to accomplish by it?—and what do *they* declare to be its *tendencies?*—but *also,* and *especially:* Does it abide the tests of God's word?—does it accord with revealed facts and principles? If it does not, then we owe it to God, to our own souls, and to our fellow-men, to reject it, as false and tending to evil; and also, in all lawful and proper ways, to convince others that their duty and their eternal interests require them to refuse it their confidence. Nor have its authors or its advocates any right to complain of such faithfulness to the truth, as unkind to them. So far from it, that it would be the very spirit of persecution, in them, to insist upon our doing otherwise.

With these views of the importance of truth, and the pernicious tendency of error, by whomsoever held or advocated, and a solemn sense of our responsibility, as those who are "*set for the defence of the Gospel,*" we design to speak plainly, and we think not *unnecessarily,* of a system now generally known by the name of "Oberlin Perfectionism." * The peculiarities of this system have now, for more than two years, been *industriously,* if not successfully urged upon the attention of many in the most of our churches, and accompanied with appeals, and suggestions, obviously tending to subvert the system of faith, and practice, heretofore adopted amongst us, and to undermine confidence, both in the settled principles of the Church, and in those who teach them and defend them. And such, meanwhile, has been our love of peace, and our anxiety to avoid even the *appearance* of unnecessary controversy, that our forbearance was beginning to be construed into approbation; or, at least, into an acknowledgement, that we could give *no reason* why these new doctrines should not be embraced, in our churches. You will perceive, then, that not a belligerent spirit, but an *urgent sense of duty,* impels us to give the following exposition, of some

* As this name (Oberlin Perfectionism) is sometimes objected to, we would say, that, in using it, we intend neither injustice nor unkindness. We wish to be *understood,* and to avoid unnecessary circumlocution. The phrase, "Modern Perfectionism," is ambiguous and indefinite. "*Christian Perfection*" is so great a favorite among several different classes of Perfectionists, that it cannot be applied as the *distinctive* and proper name of the Oberlin system. Besides, Christian candor no more requires us to concede this name to the system under consideration, than it does, that of Christians to the Chrystians; or of Disciples to the Campbellites. We use the name "Oberlin Perfectionism," because it expresses unambiguously what we intend.

of the peculiarities and tendencies of the system, to which we have adverted.

We have no disposition to say anything, in unkindness, even now; and we trust that Messrs. Finney and Mahan, at least, will not consider it uncharitable, in us, to treat their *system* even as unsparingly as they have been accustomed of late to treat ours—the system which they themselves once held, and which has been received by the great and good of so many generations. In speaking of their peculiar sentiments, we are not aware of being under the slightest temptation to do them injustice, by misstatement. Our heart's desire is, to be kind to them, just to their theory, and true to our responsibilities as ministers and Christians. The evidence upon which we rely, consists *mainly*, of their own abundant disclosures, in President Mahan's Book on Christian Perfection, and in Prof. Finney's Lectures and Letters published in the Oberlin Evangelist. It is not our purpose, or our wish, to take advantage of an occasional expression, uttered in haste; but to exhibit those sentiments upon which they greatly insist; and which they evidently regard as prominent and favorite points in their system.

SOME THINGS WHICH ARE NOT PECULIAR TO "OBERLIN PERFECTIONISM."

To guard against misapprehension, we will first mention some things, which make no part of the *peculiarities* of their system.

1st. *The doctrine, that men, as moral agents, possess all the natural faculties necessary to keep the Divine Law.*

This sentiment, so far from being peculiar to them, has been received, generally, among Christians, in all ages of the Church. The *inference* from this doctrine, viz. that men *do* perfectly keep the Divine Law, may be one of their peculiarities; yet we would not charge, even them, with holding the absurdity, that *ability* to do a thing, implies the *actual doing of that thing*. If it did imply this, then it would follow, that all moral agents every where, not excepting "the devil and his angels," perfectly keep the Divine Law.

2d. *Nor is the belief peculiar to them, that God commands all men to be perfect, and that they ought to be perfect.*

Many others, quite as much as they, contend that the Moral Law is still binding upon all men every where; and is the standard of obligation, and of perfection. If they have any peculiarity touching this point, it must consist in arguing, that because God *commands*, men *do perfectly obey:* yet we believe that even they shrink from taking a position so obviously untenable; and admit, that the mere existence of Divine commands, and of obligation resting upon all men perfectly to obey, proves absolutely nothing, in respect to the question of *actual obedience.* Surely there is such a thing, as "the heart of the sons of men being fully set in them to do evil," and their "having," universally, "no fear of God before their eyes," notwithstanding the *commands* of Jehovah, and their obligation, as moral agents, perfectly to obey them. But for the mere grace of God—notwithstanding those commands, and notwithstanding men's natural ability, and undiminished obligation—every son and daughter of Adam would, instead of being sinless, persist forever in a state of entire alienation from God. The existence of a rule of *duty,* then, proves nothing, one way or the other, in respect to its being, ar not being, actually obeyed. So that God's *commanding* men to be perfect—though it may imply natural ability, and obligation to be so—no more proves that *some* are perfect, than it does that *all* are so. That is, it proves too much, or it proves nothing.

3d. *Nor is the sentiment peculiar to them, that if men sin, it is their own fault, and that all ought to cease at once and forever from sin.*

This is, and always has been, the sentiment of evangelical Christians. But this no more proves that *some* actually attain to "a state of sinless perfection, in the *progress* of the present life," than that *all* do. For it is no more certainly the *duty* of *some,* than it is of *all,* to become sinlessly perfect. It therefore proves too much, or it proves nothing, in respect to *actual* cessation from all sin.

4th. *Nor is the sentiment peculiar to them, that none can enter Heaven, in their sins.*

Among orthodox Christians, this principle is settled beyond dispute. God, by his own express word, has established, forever, the doctrine, that whom it is his purpose to save, *he effectually calls, justifies, sanctifies, and finally glorifies.* But this no more proves that *some* attain to "a state of entire sanctification during the progress of this life," than that *all* do, who are ever admitted into Heaven. For, *in the nature of things,* it is no more necessary that *some* of God's elect should live, during their pilgrimage here, in "a state of sinless perfection," than that *all* should, in order to be admitted into "the saint's eternal rest." In respect to the degree of sanctification absolutely *requisite* for admission into Heaven, Mr. Finney's standard is certainly not *any higher,* than that of most evangelical Christians. According to him, some—not among "the least of saints" in Heaven—died, without having received the Holy Spirit, in such a measure as to "*produce the.*

entire sanctification of the soul." In the O. Evan. vol. 1, p. 138, he says: *"The thing that Abraham, and the Old Testament saints, did not receive, was that measure of the Holy Spirit which constitutes the New Covenant, and produces the Entire Sanctification of the soul."*—"It must not be supposed, that every Christian has, of course, received the Holy Ghost, in such a sense, as it is promised, in these passages;" i. e. (as he argues) *in the sense of producing entire sanctification;* "or in *any higher sense than he was received by the Old Testament saints,* who had actually been regenerated, and were real saints, of whom it is said, that 'they all died in faith, *not having received the promises;'*" i. e. (as the connection shows that *he* understands the phrase,) *not having received the blessing of entire sanctification.* And he adds: "Now it would seem as if there were *thousands of Christians who have not received the promises,* on account of their ignorance, and unbelief."

Abraham, then, and the Old Testament saints, and thousands of Christians, have died, without having "received *that measure* of the Holy Spirit, which constitutes the New Covenant, and and *produces the Entire Sanctification of the soul!"* So Mr. Finney repeatedly says; and if he does not mean what he says, then his meaning can have no relevancy to the avowed object of his argument, viz. to show that, *"under the Old Dispensation, the Holy Ghost was neither promised, nor enjoyed, to such an extent as he is promised and enjoyed, under the New Dispensation."*

Now, if we admit that Abraham, the constituted father of the faithful, on whose bosom Lazarus reclines in Paradise— that Moses, and Isaiah, and Daniel, were somewhat more blest, than Mr. Finney here seems to suppose;—if we admit that they *did* receive, just before their transition into the state of "*spirits of just men* MADE PERFECT," such a measure of the Holy Spirit, as to *complete* the work previously begun, and far advanced in them; such as to "*produce the entire sanctification of the soul*— yet, surely, we are not to infer from the *necessity of holiness as a qualification for Heaven,* that *all do,* or that *any do,* in the progress of this life, and long before the close of probation, "attain to a state of entire sanctification." It is no more true of *some,* than it is of *all* the saved, that *"they cannot enter Heaven, in their sins."* Therefore, this no more proves that *some* Christians attain to a "state of entire sanctification in the progress of this life," than it does, that *all* do. If it proves anything, at all, in relation to this point, it proves, that *none* ever enter Heaven, who have not, in the progress of this life, "*received that measure of the Holy Spirit, which produces the entire sanctification of the soul.*" But this would exclude Abraham, and all the Old Testament saints, and thousands of Christians, of whom we have reason to hope better things, from Heaven!

SOME OF THE PECULIARITIES, OR DISTINGUISHING FEATURES OF THE SYSTEM.

1st. *The doctrine, that a State of Entire Sanctification, is actually attained in the Progress of this life.*

The real point at issue, between them, and the great mass of Christians, is not—as we have seen—whether man, as a moral agent, might, with all his powers serve God, *if he were rightly disposed;* nor is it whether, in view of the provisions of the Gospel, a Christian might be in a state of entire sanctification, if he would, in fact, exercise *continually, perfect* faith in God, and *actually* come up, without any intermission, to all the requirements of the Lord Jesus Christ. To doubt that he might, would be the same as doubting that he would be entirely sanctified, *if he he were entirely sanctified.* The question is: *Do any, in fact, attain, "during the progress of the present life," to "a confirmed state of pure and perfect holiness"—of "entire obedience to the Moral Law?"* Mr. Finney and Mr. Mahan labor most zealously to prove that persons *have attained*—that persons *do attain*—to a state, in this life, of "entire sanctification," of "perfect obedience to the Moral Law," of "consecration of their whole being to Christ,"—to "a state implying the entire absence of all selfishness, and the perpetual and all pervading influence of pure and perfect love,"—to a state in which they are "morally just as perfect as God;" "actuated by the same feeling, and acting on the same principles, that God acts upon; leaving self out of the question, as uniformly as he does; being as much separated from selfishness as he is; in a word, being, in their measure, as perfect as God is." (See Mr. Mahan's Book, pp. 10, 45, and Mr. Finney's volume of Lectures to Christians, p. 253, and Oberlin Evangelist, vol. 2, p. 35.) And from individuals, who have been in a situation to know personally the facts in the case, we learn, that a considerable number of persons, at Oberlin, have been led to believe, that they *are themselves entirely sanctified*—that they come up, fully and perfectly, to *all* the requirements of God's law, "so as to live as free from all sin, as did our Lord Jesus Christ."

The notion, that a state of entire sanctification, of sinless perfection, *is actually attained during the progress of this life, is the real, distinctive feature of their system,* and *its characterizing peculiarity.* And the accumulation of proof, to establish *another* point—not in dispute—viz. that perfection in holiness, or entire sanctification, is (in the sense above explained) *attainable,* can avail nothing, in respect to the real question at issue; viz. is a state of "perfect obedience to the Moral Law," "a confirmed state of pure and perfect love," "a state of entire sanctification," *actually* attained during the progress of the present life? What Christians *ought*, morally, to be, is admitted to be made certain in the word of God. *This, then, is not a question in debate.* The point—*the distinctive principle*—which Mr. Finney and Mr. Mahan labor to establish, is, that a state of sinless perfection, *is actually attained*, in the progress of this life.

Apology for teaching this doctrine of Sinless Perfection actually attained: "*What harm can it do, if we hold up the Moral Law as the standard of Perfection?*"—*But is that Law likely to be held up fully and faithfully, by persons advocating this doctrine?*

In apology for this leading doctrine of their system, its authors strenuously insist, that its tendency cannot be injurious, *whilst* they continue to hold up the Divine Law, as the standard of perfection. By this, they seem to admit, that its tendency must be injurious, *if the law of God be not, in all its spirituality and broadness of claim, held up, and clearly apprehended, as the unchanging standard of Perfection.*

Yes, they say: "*if the proper standard be only held up.*"— Very well: suppose this were conceded. Now look at the law as distinctly as you can. Contemplate it, just as it is, in the unabated strictness and broadness of its demands: "Thou shalt love the Lord thy God with all thy heart, and with all thy soul, and with all thy might," "and thy neighbor as thyself." To aid your conception of its spirituality, and the extent of its claims, compare with it, some of the very best specimens of human attainment. Behold, first, a long list of Old Testament saints. Behold Job, whom Christians are commanded (Jas. 5, 10, 11) to "take for an *ensample* of suffering affliction and patience;" and Abraham, the Mirror of Faith, equivocating, nevertheless, once and again, through distrust of a protecting Providence; and Moses, the Proverb of Meekness, "angered at the waters of strife," and "provoked to speak unadvisedly with his lips;" and Isaiah, "the Evangelical Prophet," crying out, in an agony of self-abasement: "Wo is me, for I am undone; because I am a man of unclean lips; for mine eyes have seen the King, the Lord of hosts;" and Elijah, "according to whose word," (1 Ki. 17: 1) "the heaven was shut up three years and six months," (Lu. 4: 25,) and then "gave rain," (Jas. 5: 18); and others, whose spiritual attainments justified Paul and James, in presenting them to *us*, who live under the New Dispensation, as illustrious models of Christian Faith, and of prevailing Prayer; and who yet "*did not* (according to a principle for which Mr. Finney contends) *receive that measure of the Holy Spirit, which produces the entire sanctification of the soul.*" And then contemplate Peter, so bold and strong in the Lord, on the day of Pentecost, and before the Sanhedrim, yet afterwards rebuked by Paul, at Antioch, for his dissimulation, "because he was to be blamed;" and Paul himself, so crucified to the world, so heavenly minded, and so abundant in labors, yet declaring, with the most emphatic repetition, his sense of remaining imperfection. "Not as though I had *already attained*, either were *already perfect.*" "Brethren, I count not myself *to have apprehended."* We cannot suppose, that the apostle meant, in these passages, to utter a truth, so perfectly *needless to the Philippians,* as that which is attributed to him, by those who labor to explain away the obvious import of these declarations. We cannot believe that, to the very faithful, and remarkably correct Philippians, he meant, *so emphatically,* to say *merely :* "Not as though—being dead and buried, and having heard the voice of the archangel, and the trump of God—I had already had my vile body fashioned like unto Christ's glorious body, or were already put in possession of an everlasting crown of righteousness, in Heaven. *Brethren* —I repeat it—*I count not myself to be already dead, and to have apprehended, beyond the tomb, the blessedness of 'just men made perfect.'* " We cannot believe, that he felt the need of saying to them *so earnestly,* and *so repeatedly,* not only that he was not yet raised up in the resurrection of the just; but also that he had not completed his course on earth—that he had not yet (being dead) *been perfected,* in the sense of *receiving, in Heaven, his everlasting crown of righteousness,* and of being in a glorified state;* but that he intended—as plain readers naturally understand him—to speak of imperfection in his spiritual attainments. So that, "forgetting the things which were behind, and reaching forth to the things that were before, he was pressing towards the mark, for the prize of the high calling of God, in Christ Jesus." Behold, too, the apostle James, "the Lord's brother," so strenuous for "*a living faith,*" yet acknowledging, that "in *many things we all offend;*" not merely *we* offend, but "we *all* offend." And John, the beloved disciple, declaring: "If we say that *we have no sin,* we deceive ourselves, and the truth is not in us;" and also, "If we say we *have not sinned,* we make Him a liar, and

* Mr. Mahan has recently tried to make it appear, that Paul was meeting the error of some who "said that the resurrection was past already." To this far-fetched idea, it is quite sufficient to object: 1. That no such error is once hinted at in this epistle. In his second epistle to Timothy, written (as Paley, Macknight and others have clearly demonstrated) at least two or three years afterwards, Paul—in illustrating the tendency of holding and teaching false doctrines—incidentally ment.ons Hymeneus and Philetus, two false teachers at Ephesus, *not Philippi,* "who (says he) concerning the truth have erred, saying that the resurrection is passed already, and overthrow the faith of *some."* Of *some :* he does not say of *many.* even at the *place where they taught,* and at the *date of the second epistle* to Timothy. (See 2 Tim. 2: 16—18.) 2. That under the circumstances, it would have been most strange and unnatural, to make such *repeated* and *emphatic* declarations, to meet this error, and yet in a way so *indirect,* and so *little likely* to be understood.

his word is not in us,"—thus distinguishing, by the use of a different tense, the delusion of those who say, they *are now in a state of sinless perfection*, from the wickedness of those who say, they *have not committed* any act of transgression. And in modern times, Whitefield, the man of eighteen thousand sermons, and praying even more than he preached, yet, to the last, confessing, with such deep feeling, his failure to meet all the demands of the Divine Law; and Prest. Edwards, with spiritual attainments, perhaps unsurpassed since the days of Paul—hear him saying, with humility so unfeigned: "I know not how to express better what my sins appear to me to be, that by heaping infinite upon infinite, and multiplying infinite by infinite."

Judging now of the elevation and strictness of the Divine Law, by comparing it, or rather contrasting it, with the lives even of such men, we would ask: Are those who have burdened themselves with the task, of sustaining the theory of *sinless perfection actually attained*, in a position to hold up faithfully and steadily, *such a standard of perfection?* Are they not under a temptation not likely to be resisted, to degrade the Divine Law—to dim the moral glory of that standard, in view of which so many holy prophets, and apostles, and other eminent saints *have confessed themselves unclean?* While laboring under the burden of their favorite assumption, that *some do perfectly obey the Moral Law*, are they not—with such samples of Christian attainment as are in fact furnished by the Church below—under not merely a strong temptation, but a sort of logical necessity, to lower down the standard, to the stubborn exigencies of human experience, so that if the experience will not suit the rule, the rule shall suit the experience? And will not a community, in which such samples of Christian experience are considered *perfect*, be naturally led to have an idea of perfection in holiness, very inferior to that which dwelt in the mind of Job—of Isaiah—of Prest. Edwards? We feel constrained, therefore, to say, that the idea is altogether preposterous, of holding such a theory for any length of time, with a clear and full apprehension, and faithful exhibition of God's Law as the standard of perfection. It cannot be long concealed, that Perfectionism, whatever may be its *pretensions or its promises*, does, and must stand rebuked before the Divine Law; and that it is, in any and every form which it may assume, *essentially Antinomian.*

2. *A Result of holding the Doctrine of Sinless Perfection Attained, viz: The sentiment that heretofore the Standard of Christian Perfection has been set much too high.*

We are not surprised that even Mr. Finney and Mr. Mahan, are yielding to the *logical necessity* of their false position, to *abate and lower down* the claims of the Moral Law. In the

O. Evan. vol. 2, p. 50, Mr. Finney says: "It is objected that this doctrine lowers the standard of holiness, to a level with our own experience. It is not denied that in some instances this may have been true. Nor can it be denied that the standard of Christian Perfection, has been elevated much above the demands of the law, in its application to human beings in our present state of existence." "To be sure, there may be danger of frittering away the claims of the Law; but I would humbly inquire, whether hitherto the error has not been on the *other side?*" Speaking of one who declared that it "was revolting to his feelings to hear any mere man set up the claim of [entire] obedience to the Law of God," he says: "I know that the brother to whom I allude, would be almost the last man deliberately and knowingly to give any strained interpretation to the Law of God; and yet I cannot but feel, that much of the difficulty that good men have upon this subject, has arisen out of a comparison of the lives of saints, with *a standard entirely above that which the Law of God does or can demand of persons in all respects in our circumstances.*" Mr. Mahan expresses the same sentiment, respecting setting the claims of the Law too high, (on p. 148 of his Book,) with something like a sneer at the zeal of Christians, concerning its demands.

3. *Another peculiarity nearly allied to the foregoing.—Mr Finney and Mr. Mahan dwell much upon the idea, that our Powers are greatly debilitated in consequence of transgression; and that therefore the Law does not and cannot claim so much of us, as it would if our faculties had not been thus weakened by sin.*

As a mere specimen of their language, on the subject of *debilitated powers,* and *diminished obligation,* we quote the following from the O. Evan. vol. 1, p. 44. Speaking of what constitutes perfect obedience to the Law of God, Mr. Finney says: "Nor does it imply that we exercise the same strength or consistency of holy affection that we might have done had we never sinned. If we love him with what strength we have, be it more or less, however debilitated our powers may be, it is all that the Law of God requires." We mention this sentiment, not so much to give an opinion of the thing itself, as to bring out the fact distinctly, that they give *this doctrine, of debilitated powers and of consequently diminished obligation, remarkable prominence, in their exposition of the demands of the Law.* Yet we would ask, if there are not involved in the doctrine itself, certain premises, from which some dangerous conclusions *might* follow? Suppose it to be true, that sin debilitates one's faculties, and by debilitating them diminishes his *obligation;* does it not follow, that sin tends to set him free from obligation to his Creator, by constantly lessening

14

the amount of love and service which he owes?—and by continuing to sin, and thus to diminish his obligation, would he not be constantly *approximating* towards the point, where his powers would be *all* wasted by transgression, and his obligation to his insulted Creator be in the same ratio reduced?

We do not charge them with holding and asserting this conclusion as a part of their creed; but is not this conclusion fairly deducible from premises which we have proved that they do hold?

4. *Another peculiarity resulting from attachment to the theory of Sinless Perfection attained.—Very slight evidence convinces Mr. Finney and Mr. Mahan, that all the demands of the Divine Law have, by certain individuals, been fully met.*

For example: they insist that Paul was in a state of sinless perfection, because in his epistles to the Churches, which he had gathered in Thessalonica, Corinth and Philippi, he directs those recent converts from heathenism—the most of them mere babes in Christ, unused to walking in the faith and order of the Gospel—to be followers of him—referring them to the holy and unblamable example which he had set whilst among them.— That is, between an example *comparatively* so holy that men see in it nothing to blame—between a *sincere purpose* of life to glorify God, and to proclaim the whole Gospel to all sorts of persons, so as, in an important sense, to be pure from the blood of all men—between this, and coming up fully to every demand of that Law which is spiritual, and its commandment exceeding broad, they *now* see no interval—no difference, even in degree. Now many a devoted missionary, making no pretension to sinless perfection, might, with evident propriety, address similar language to churches which he had been instrumental of gathering in heathen lands. Yet, says Mr. Finney (O. Evan. vol. 2, p. 35): "*If Paul was not sinless, he was an extravagant boaster; and such language, used by any minister in these days, would be considered as the language of an extravagant boaster.*" Paul's "unblamableness" of deportment is greatly relied upon, as showing that he was in a state of entire sanctification. Yet, even before his conversion, he was, "touching the righteousness which is in the law, *blameless*," (Phil. 3: 6,) though utterly destitute of holiness, in the sight of God. In Luke 1: 6, we are told, that "Zacharias was righteous before God, walking in all the commandments and ordinances of the Lord *blameless*." Now why do they not exult over this strong proof-text, the strongest in the New Testament, for their theory of sinless perfection? "Zacharias was RIGHTEOUS—BEFORE GOD—WALKING IN ALL THE COMMANDMENTS—AND ORDINANCES OF THE LORD—BLAMELESS." Why not say of this, too, " If it does not express a state of entire sanctification, then it is not in the power of language to express such an idea?" Why insist so much on *other* passages, and say so little of this *stronger one?* Is it because Zacharias lived under the Old Dispensation, when the saints "did not receive that measure of the Holy Spirit which produces the entire sanctification of the soul?"—or because we are informed (compare 20, 62 vs.) that Gabriel not only censured him for his unbelief, but announced a chastisement for the sin, consisting in the loss of speech, and of hearing, for nine months? This argument, from "blamelessness," or "unblamableness," then, proves too much, or it proves nothing for their theory.

Paul's "sincerity," too, is greatly relied on, as showing that he must have been in a state of entire conformity to God's Law. Mr. Mahan (on p. 47 of his Book) quotes a *part* of 1 Cor. 4: 4, in proof: "I know nothing by myself, i.'e. I am *conscious of no wrong;*" though the apostle immediately adds: "*yet am I not hereby justified,*" and thus at a blow demolishes the very position which Mr. wishes to establish by the other clause of the verse. See Acts 26: 9. Mr. Finney and Mr. Mahan labor, too, to show that Paul, and some others, were sinless, because the apostle, after saying so emphatically, (Phil. 3: 12, 13:) "Not as though I had already attained, either were already perfect," "Brethren, I count not myself to have apprehended," says in the 15th verse: "Let us therefore, *as many as be perfect,* be thus minded." Their exegesis amounts to this, that Paul was, in one sense, imperfect,—in another, perfect; that when he said he "had not already attained," he meant that he had not yet been called forth from his grave to the resurrection of life; and that when he said: "Not as though I were already perfect," he meant, "not as though I had finished my course on earth, and had already received a crown of righteousness in the world of glory;", but that when he said, "let us therefore, as many as be perfect," etc., he meant to imply that himself, and some in the Philippian Church had attained to a state of sinless perfection. It is worthy of remark, that few commentators, of any respectability, whatever might be their theory, have ventured to give such an interpretation to this passage. Even Dr. Adam Clark—whose zeal to sustain a theory, bearing, in one or two points, some resemblance to Oberlin Perfectionism, was only a *little less* than that of the Oberlin Professors, to uphold theirs—gives a different meaning to the word "perfect," in this verse. We quote his note, not because we have peculiar confidence, at least, in his *opinions,* but because *his* interpretation of the passage is to be regarded as a *concession to obvious truth.*

"Phil. 3:15. *As many as be perfect.*] *As many as are thoroughly instructed in Divine things.*—The word Teleioi, *perfect,* is taken here in the same sense in which it is taken in 1 Cor. 14: 20: Be not children in understanding, but in understanding be ye men; Teleioi Ginesthe; *be ye perfect*, thoroughly instructed, deeply experienced. 1 Cor. 2: 6, *We speak wisdom among the perfect;* En Tois Teleiois; among those who are fully instructed, *adults* in Christian knowledge. Eph. 4: 13, Till we all come unto a perfect man; His Andra Teleion; to the state of *adults* in Christianity. Heb. 5: 14, *But strong me belongeth to them that are of full age;* Teleion; *the perfect,* they who are *thoroughly* instructed and experienced in Divine things. *Let us therefore,* says the apostle, *as many as be perfect*—as have entered fully into the spirit and design of the Gospel, *be thus minded.*"

We do not wonder at the anxiety of Mr. Finney and Mr. Mahan, to prove that *Paul* was entirely sanctified. For if *he* was not, then the pretensions of those who now claim to be sinlessly perfect, must be, to say the least, of a very suspicious character. But it is not too much to say, that their effort to do this, while it has proved an entire failure, has manifested a zeal to sustain their darling assumption, which poorly qualifies them for the needful task of holding up faithfully the Divine Law as the standard of perfection. Can it be possible that any should have elevated and correct views of that *transcript* of God's moral nature, and at the same time have so evident a predisposition to be convinced, by slender proofs, that all of its claims are perfectly met; and met, too, by individuals of that race whose character and moral propensities are described so fearfully in the word of God? What is there in the Bible, whether in relation to man as he is by nature, or to man as he is in a state of grace, to justify so ready a belief, that he actually attains to a state of sinless perfection in the progress of this life? 1 . i. 8: 46, *"For there is no man that sinneth not."* Eccl. 7: 20, *"For there is not a just man upon earth, that doeth good and sinneth not."* Jas. 3:2, *"For in many things we offend all,* i. e. we all offend." 1 John 1: 8, *"If we say that we have no sin, we deceive ourselves, and the truth is not* ." 1 John 3: 3, *"And every man that hath this hope in him purifieth himself even as he is pure."* Is it true of any man, in whom the work of sanctification is *already completed,* that he purifieth himself—that, with the sinless character of Christ before his mind, as the standard, he *is now laboring in the work of purifying himself,* even as he is pure? This text, with the preceding, Macknight regards as "overthrowing the Pelagian notion, that good men may live without sin, *and that many good men have actually so lived."* Prov. 20: 9, *"Who can say I have made my heart clean—I am pure from my sin?"* Gal. 5: 17, *"For the flesh lusteth against the Spirit, and the Spirit against the flesh: and there are contrary the one to the other; so that ye cannot do the things that ye would."* Heb. 12: 7—11, *"If ye endure chastening, God dealeth with you as with sons; for what son is he whom the*

Father chasteneth not? But if ye be without chastisement, whereof all are partakers, then are ye bastards, and not sons. Furthermore, we have had fathers of our flesh, which corrected us; and we gave them reverence: shall we not much rather be in subjection unto the Father of spirits, and live? For they verily for a few days chastened us after their own pleasure; but he for our profit, that we might be partakers of his holiness. Now no chastening for the present seemeth to be joyous, but grievous: nevertheless, afterward it yieldeth the peaceable fruit of righteousness unto them which are exercised thereby." The object of God's disciplinary dealings with his children, as here described, is to sanctify them—to cause "those who are exercised thereby to yield the peaceable fruits of righteousness." Does God so delight in afflicting his children, that he continues to employ the "grievous" means upon those who have already taken perfectly his moral image? Can it be possible, then, that any become, in the progress of this life, "morally just as perfect as God"—that any attain to "a state implying the entire absence of all selfishness, and the perpetual and all-pervading influence of pure and perfect love?"—to "a confirmed state of pure and perfect holiness, such as the Moral Law demands?" What could be the object of inflicting chastisement upon *such*—that *"chastisement whereof all are partakers?"* An effort, which, in respect to zeal and determination, may remind some persons of the labors of Universalian exegesis, has been made, to give to these passages a meaning consistent with the theory of sinless perfection attained; and the lack, even of plausibility, in most of the expositions given, indicates the unscriptural nature of the theory, for the sake of which the effort was made. This shows, and is mentioned only to show, how far the judgment even of *well-intending* men may be misled by attachment to a false theory.

5. Another Peculiarity.—*That which first leads people to sin, is their Innocent Constitution, just as it was the Innocent Constitution of Adam, to which the temptation was addressed, that led him to sin.**

This is Mr. Finney's own sentiment, expressed in his own words. He takes great pains to show not only that sanctification implies merely "present obedience," "right volitions now," and produces "no change of our nature so that we become good in ourselves," but that there is nothing "in us," antecedent to

* Pelagius said: "The state of man before the fall was the same as it is now." "The sin of Adam is not original in relation to his posterity. Every one who comes after him, is born into the world as pure and free as Adam was created, and in a less advantageous position, only, in respect of the weakness of infancy, and the necessity of growing up under the influence of sinful example."

moral action, operating as the *occasion* of sinful exercises, which *needs* to be either eradicated or *changed* in order to our being in a state of entire sanctification. Take the following, instead of many passages which might be quoted. O. Evan. vol. 2, p. 2, Speaking of some one, who said that a person might now avoid all transgression, and yet not be in a state of entire sanctification, because there might be that in him "which would lay the foundation for his sinning at a future time," viz. "that which first led him to sin at the beginning of his moral existence," Mr. Finney says: "I answered, that that which first led him to sin was his *innocent constitution, just as* it was the *innocent constitution* of Adam, to which the temptation was addressed, that led him into sin. Adam's *innocent constitutional appetites*, when excited by the presence of objects fitted to excite them, were a sufficient temptation to lead him to consent to prohibited indulgence, which constituted his sin. *Now just so it certainly is with every human being.*" *

---

* "Pelagius, in dwelling too intensely upon the inherent freedom of man, overlooked the possibility of a corruption derived by natural generation, without impairing that freedom. He analyzed too exclusively one faculty of our being. This was his great philosophical error.

"Man can will both good and evil. So far he was correct. But the consequence which he drew—therefore man can *be* good or evil—is not legitimate. Man has intelligence, and therefore he can know. He has will, and therefore he can choose and do. But it does not follow, that because he has affections of love and hate. he can direct these affections to any object known by his intelligence and selected by his will. The intelligence may affirm what objects *ought* to be loved, and what objects *ought* to be hated: and the will may direct the whole attention to the contemplation of these objects and their qualities, and call up any known influence within its reach, that may conduce to the required affection: but the affection itself can no more be a creation of the will, than a perception of the intelligence.

"It is a fact of universal consciousness, that the affections of man are, in many important points, opposed to the decisions of reason and conscience. While this opposition exists, man cannot be called good in a perfect sense."

"Now, let it be supposed that an individual, up to a given moment, has, in every personal act. obeyed the reason and denied his impure propensities: it is not philosophically conceivable that he has incurred any guilt on account of the mere existence of these propensities: on the contrary, his virtues have taken a nobler cast from the stern resistance to temptation under which they were moulded. But is he perfectly good? No. The evil element is within him; and therefore we know not but the next demand of conscience may be one which he shall choose to disobey. He contains perpetually within his own nature motives to transgression.

"Two forms of evil are found in man: the evil of a depraved moral sensitivity, or a sensitivity at war with reason, wherein lie motives, temptations and inducements to personal or free acts of sin: and the evil of positive acts of the free will, transgressing the law of conscience. Pelagius obtained his perfect man, by shutting out of view the first form of evil, and concentrating his idea in the second. If it were not for the first, in the absolute freedom of the will, perfection would seem an easy attainment. But inasmuch as the first is continually present, until perfection is actually gained—besides the bare possibility of sin which attaches itself to the free will—there is the probability arising from the subjective motives lying in the sensitivity.

In relation to this subject, we would remark, 1st. No intelligent Christian believes that entire sanctification implies the creation of any new natural faculty, or the annihilation of any
susceptibility, appetite, or propensity, which belonged to man as
he was when "*God made him upright;*" nor is it "the perfection
of candor," to ascribe such a sentiment to any branch of the
Church of Christ. In respect to this point there is, there can
be no ground for controversy. We remark, 2dly. That the
meaning of the above declaration of Mr. Finney is evident from
the professed object which he had in view, i. e. to *refute* the
doctrine, that apart from present transgression, "there might
be that in a person which would lay the foundation for his sinning at a future time," viz. "that which first led him to sin, at
the beginning of his moral existence." The existence of native
depravity, or of any propensity to sin, or susceptibility to be led
into sin, except what belonged equally to Adam before the fall,
is by Mr. Finney most distinctly and emphatically denied.

"*That which first led him to sin was his innocent constitution,*"

The man is never deprived of responsibility, because he is never deprived of
free will—the power of striving after self-regeneration; but the probability of
transgression found in his depraved faculty, exemplified in the history of so
many generations, has grown to a moral certainty. Christianity made her
appearance after the long experiment of ages had been made upon unaided
human nature: she did not dispute or set aside the philosophical grounds of
responsibility, and the capacity of man to choose the good, and seek the
highest possible elevation of his being. She assumed these; and, without
waiting any longer for *what he might do*, she took up the facts of *what he had
done*, and brought in a glorious and efficient remedy for the evils of which he
had failed to relieve himself.

"Pelagius, therefore, not only failed in his anthropological and psycholog-
ical analysis; he failed also in perceiving the just relations of Christianity,
considered as a system of truth, to philosophy in general; and its universal
and intense necessity, considered as a remedy for human guilt and fallibility.
In *doing away* from human nature all fixed depravity, and in resolving the
recovery of moral purity into *obedient acts of the will*, he did away the necessity of the supe.natural influences of the Holy Spirit. He indeed believed
that these influences were actually given: but they were given, not as indis-
pensable to holiness, but as enabling the Christian to attain to higher degrees
of holiness than were possible without them."

"The legitimate tendencies of Pelagianism, theoretically considered, are
in some points highly dangerous. It may be granted, in Christian charity,
that Pelagius was himself a good man: it must be acknowledged, also, that
his representations of the freedom and ability of man are calculated to quicken
the sense of responsibility, and to rouse to great activity in duty. But, in
removing the attention from an inherent depravity, and insisting upon the
sinlessness of some men, and in giving the influences of the Holy Spirit only
a secondary place in the work of sanctification, his system would naturally
cause men to think lightly of the moral evils of the world—encourage a false
security, and lead to self-deception—introduce a confident self-reliance, to
the neglect of prayer for the Holy Spirit—and beget self-righteousness, instead of humility, penitence and faith. The historical results have but too
faithfully realized the theoretical tendencies."—*Prof. Henry Tappan's Review
of Wigger's History of Augustinism and Pelagianism, Am. Bib. Repos. Jan,
1841, pp. 218, '19, '20, '21.*

just as it was the innocent constitution of Adam to which the temptation was addressed that led him into sin!" Is this, we ask, the doctrine of the Bible, that what first leads us into sin is our *constitution*, and that an "*innocent* constitution?"—that there is nothing in our *fallen nature* which needs change in order to our being in a state of entire sanctification?—that "every human being" is led into sin by *just such innocent constitutional appetites as belonged to Adam before his first sin?* Rom. 5: 12, "*By one man sin entered into the world,*" i. e. the sin of Adam was, in a *peculiar sense*, the occasion of universal human depravity. John 3: 6, "*That which is born of the flesh is flesh.*" "By *that which is born of the flesh,*" says Barnes, " he (Christ) evidently intends man as he is by nature, in the circumstances of his natural birth."—"*Is flesh.* Partakers of the nature of the parent. Compare Gen. 5: 3. As the parents are corrupt and sinful, so will be their descendants. See Job 14: 4. As the parents are *wholly* corrupt by *nature,* so their children will be the same. The word *flesh* here is used to denote *corrupt, defiled, sinful.*" That there is in man now, something leading to sin more than "innocent constitutional appetites," such as belonged to Adam before the fall, is evident from such passages as the following. Rom. 7: 5, "For when we were in the flesh, the *motions of sins.* (literally *the passions of sins.* i. e. *sinful passions,*) which were by the law, (i. e. excited in the unrenewed heart by the restraints of the Holy Law.) did *work in our members to bring forth fruit unto death;*" see Barnes in loco. Rom. 7: 9, "*But sin* (not "innocent constitutional appetites." just like unfallen Adam's) taking *occasion* by the commandment. *wrought in me all manner of concupiscence.*" Rom. 7: 21, " I find then a *law,* that when I would do good *evil* (not an " innocent constitution," exactly; but, says Barnes, some *corrupt desire,* or *improper feeling,* or *evil propensity*) is present with me." " The sense," according to Barnes, " is, that to do evil is agreeable to our strong natural inclinations and passions." We need scarcely to remark, that whether we consider the 7th of Rom. as written of regenerate or of unregenerate character, makes no difference with the force of these passages, in relation to the point now in question. See also Ps. 51: 5; 2 Pet. 2: 19; Eph. 2: 3; 4: 22; 1 Ti. 6: 5; and as showing that sanctification implies a work more deep and rad cal than *the mere regulation of present acts of the will,* compare Ps. 51: 10; 2 Cor. 5: 17; Eph. 2: 10; Rom. 12: 2; 2 Cor. 3: 18, etc.

We cannot refrain from noticing here, the unwarrantable use which Mr. Finney and his coadjutors make of Heb. 4: 15, to sustain their denial of *native depravity.* or of a strong hereditary propensity to sin, in the posterity of Adam. "*All the susceptibilities of our nature,*" says he, "Christ must have had, or he could not have been " *tempted in all points like as we are.*"

Now it is remarkable, that in the original of this passage, there is a most careful guarding, by the apostle, against the very idea which Mr. Finney evidently wishes to derive from it. It is very literally translated by Dr. Macknight: " was tempted in all points *according to the likeness* [of his nature to ours] without sin." His note is: " The likeness of our Lord's nature to ours, was was *not an exact likeness;* for he was free from *that corruption* which, as the consequence of Adam's sin, has infected all mankind." Dr. Adam Clark's excellent remark upon this passage is the more highly appreciated for the reason already given. " The words Kata Panta Kath' Omoioteta, might be translated, "*in all points according to the likeness,*" i. e. as far as his human nature could bear affinity to ours; for though he had a perfect human body and human soul, yet that body was perfectly tempered; it was free from all morbid action, and consequently from all *irregular movements.* His *mind,* or *human soul,* being free from all sin, being every way perfect, could feel no *irregular temper,* nothing inconsistent with infinite purity. *In all these respects he was different from us, and cannot, as man, sympathize with us in feelings of this kind.*"

That Mr. Finney infers too much from Heb. 4: 15, is evident from Christ's own declaration. (John 14: 30.) " For the prince of this world cometh, and *hath nothing in me.*" i. e (according to Barnes) " there is in me no principle or feeling that accords with his, and nothing, therefore, by which the adversary can prevail." " As Jesus had no *such evil principle;* as he was not at all under the influence of any native depravity, or attachment to forbidden objects, so Satan had nothing in him, and could not prevail." These words express the common and obvious view of the passage—the very same that is taken of it by Doddridge, Scott, Adam Clark, and others.

The denial of what is understood by native depravity, or a propensity to sin consequent upon the apostacy of Adam, is not only unscriptural but unphilosophical. It is irreconcilable with facts, and facts, too, which are admitted by Mr. Finney himself, and those who are associated with him.

The *fact* is admitted, that mankind without exception sin, and only sin, (previous to regeneration,) from the very moment when they begin to act with any knowledge of a rule of duty. How then shall this *universal* sinfulness, so *entire* in each individual of the human family, be accounted for? By saying that men are free agents, and therefore *can* sin if they choose? As free agents, they *can* obey God if they choose. The mere fact of their being free agents, no more implies their universal *sinfulness* than it does their universal *holiness.* The angels in Heaven are free agents, and they are all holy. Free agency, therefore, though it may imply the *possibility* of sin, cannot be

the cause or the occasion of the *universal* and *total* sinfulness
of mankind. Is the power of education, social influence, or the
principle of imitation, sufficient to account for such a fact?
Why, then, are *all* the children of the most pious parents, sinners and totally destitute of holiness? Why are the children of
such parents, even when bred up in the midst of a community
almost entirely pious, where all or nearly all the parental, social, and even "physiological" influences may be assumed to
be favorable to holiness, and where "*the very atmosphere seems
religious;*" why are even those children such that they need to
be told that He who "now commandeth *all* men *everywhere* to
repent," says to them also, "except *ye repent, ye shall all like-
wise perish?*" If the fact of being free agents, and witnessing
the transgressions of other free agents, can account for *the universal* and *total* sinfulness of the many millions of mankind, why
did not "the child Jesus" become a sinner in the wicked city of
Nazareth? And why have none of the angels become corrupt-
ed, who have had to do with the affairs of this world; e. g. those
two who spent a night with Lot in Sodom, and conducted him
forth from that abode of abominations?

Let no one imagine that this unscriptural doctrine, avowed so
repeatedly and distinctly in the Oberlin Evangelist, has the confidence or the support of those Christians who are sometimes
called the "New School," but are *better* known as Constitutional
Presbyterians, or as New England Congregationalists, that, in
respect to Theology, sympathize with them. To say nothing of
the sentiments of Dr. Beecher, and other eminent men of kindred
views, the truth of this assertion is evinced by the most explicit
declarations of Albert Barnes and Moses Stuart, who will not,
by any candid person, be accused of a bias towards hyper-ortho-
doxy, in relation to this point. Mr. Barnes declares: "I mean
to say, that there is *something* which I do not profess myself
able to explain, *antecedent* to the *moral action* of the posterity
of Adam, and *growing out of the relation which they sustain to
him, as the head of the race,* which *makes it certain* that they
will sin as soon as they begin to act as moral agents, however
early that may be. This *hereditary tendency* to sin, I suppose,
is what has usually been called "original sin;" and the existence of this I have not denied, but have always affirmed, and
do now most firmly hold. What the precise metaphysical nature of this is, I do not pretend to know."—"*Men are indubitably affected by the sin of Adam,* as e. g. *by being born with a
corrupt disposition; with loss of righteousness,*" etc. See Barnes'
Defence, pp. 174, 175.

Prof. Stuart remarks: "I believe the susceptibility of impression from sinful and enticing objects, belongs to the *tout ensemble* of our nature; not to the body exclusively, nor to the soul

exclusively, but, from their essential and intimate and wonderful connection, to the *tout ensemble* of both, i. e. to man. I believe this susceptibility is innate, connate, original, natural, native, or whatever else one may please to call it, by way of thus characterizing it. I believe that it commences with our being, in a sense like to that in which an oak tree commences with the acorn. I believe this susceptibility to be such, that just as soon as there is growth and maturity enough for development, it will develope itself in persuading or influencing men—all men—to sin. I believe this to be the natural state of *fallen* man; while in his original state, before the fall, the predominant tendency of his susceptibilities was just the *reverse* of what it now is."— "Infants are to be saved from the direful effects of the fall of Adam. Ever since that fall, their nature is degraded in some highly important respects."—"Pelagius said that they were, while very young, like to Adam in his original state of innocence. I am no Pelagian; I do not believe at all in this position. *I think it to be radically and fundamentally erroneous.*—"In Adam the virtuous susceptibilities (if I may so speak, in order to characterize susceptibilities concerned in inclining him to virtuous action) were, beyond all question, strongly predominant. They remained so until his fall. *But in infants now, the case is wholly reversed.*" See Bib. Repos. for July, 1839, pp. 43, 45, 48.

Quite as little sympathy, touching *this* point, at least, will the authors of "Oberlin Perfectionism," receive from Arminian or Wesleyan Methodists. In their "Articles of Religion," they say: "Original sin standeth not in *the following* of Adam, (as the Pelagians do vainly talk,) but it is the corruption of the nature of every man, that naturally is engendered of the offspring of Adam, whereby man is very far gone from original righteousness, and of his own nature inclined to evil, and that continually." See Book of Discipline, pp. 11, 12.

We have dwelt the longer upon this subject, because an error of such importance, in relation to human depravity, may be expected, sooner or later, to affect and greatly to modify all the doctrinal views of those who hold it; because it has, in fact, done much to give to the Oberlin theory of sanctification its distinctive features; and also because the real "position" of its advocates, in relation to the Bible, in relation to sound philosophy, and also in relation to the known sentiments of the visible Church, ought to be clearly "defined."

6. *The term Flesh, where it is used to denote Corrupt Human Nature, or the Carnal Man, made to signify mere subjection to Bodily Appetites, i. e. bad Dietetic habits, etc.—Prospect of the Flesh being, by Physiological Reform, overcome entirely,*

and the Human Body, in a few generations, completely Renovated and Restored to its Primitive Physical Perfection.

It is not our province, here, to inquire *how* the term *sarx,* flesh, *came* tropically to denote *the carnal man, the unrenewed heart*—or the *dreadful moral diathesis of human nature resulting from the original apostasy.* That it *has,* in a large class of important passages, this signification, is so very evident as rarely to be denied. Pres. Dwight declares, that, in scripture usage, it has *"customarily"* this meaning. It is sometimes applied to the totally unrenewed nature of the unconverted, and sometimes to the "remainders" of corruption in Christians. Read in their connection, e, g. John. 3: 6; Rom. 7: 5, 18; 8: 1, 6, 13; and 1 Cor. 3: 3; Gal. 5: 17. An accurate comparison of Mark 7: 21—23, with Gal. 5: 19—21, shows not only that the term flesh denotes something *more* than subjection to bodily appetites—than bad *physiological habits;* but that it corresponds very nearly, if not precisely, in its *range of corrupt exercises.* with the natural heart of man. Doubtless no inconsiderable *part* of human corruption and vileness, is manifested in the influence of the bodily appetites upon the exercises of the mind, and *in the influence of the imagination in inflaming passions having their seat in the body.* The only question is, can what is said of the *flesh*—of being *in the flesh*—of *walking after the flesh*—and of *the works of the flesh*—be all resolved into mere *subjection of the soul to bodily appetites—into intemperance—into wrong physiological habits?* And can *all* that our Saviour (in John 3: 6) and that Paul (in Rom. 7: 18, or in Gal. 5: 17—23) intended by the term *flesh,* be done away among men, in a few generations, by *physiological reform."* That it cannot, is certain. Among the works of the *flesh.* Paul mentions *hatred, variance, emulations, wrath, strife, seditions. envyings, murders.* i. e. exercises of *mind,* which have characterized not only Pharisees, Cynics, Stoics, Anchorites, and Eunuchs, but *devils,* or *fallen spirits—* none of whose sins can be imputed to *wrong physiological habits.* If it should be said, that he also mentions adultery. fornication, uncleanness, etc. we remark, that this is perfectly consistent with our view of the subject, viz. that these are *some* of the sins to which the *carnal man* is prone. But if we are to conclude from this, that the *flesh* denotes mere subjection to bodily appetites, then must we conclude, also, that the natural *heart* signifies the same thing. For out of the *heart* proceed not only evil thoughts, murders, covetousness, deceit, envy and' pride, but also adulteries, fornications and lasciviousness. Paul declared (1 Cor. 3: 3) that those "babes" in Christ at Corinth, were carnal, sarkikoi, fleshly, *because* there were among them—not wrong *physiological* habits exactly—but "*envying, and strife, and divisions."* That is, an *ambitious, contentious spirit* among them was evidence, and the evidence which, the Holy Ghost suggested to the apostle, as showing that they were yet, in no small measure, *carnal*. Can it be that the apostle intended to say, that a class of sins, which exist in a far greater degree in *fallen spirits*, than among *men*, proved that those Christians were in subjection to *bodily appetites?* It may be that they *were so*, in a measure; but did their " *envying and strife and divisions*," alone, *prove* it? In short, "flesh" and "spirit," to " walk after the flesh," and to " walk after the Spirit," " the works of the flesh," and " the fruit of the Spirit," " the minding of the flesh," and " the minding of the Spirit," etc. are expressions obviously denoting the exact and entire opposite of each other—the one implying whatever, in man, is not conformed to the Law of God; the other whatever, in man, is the result of the Holy Spirit's transforming agency. Whenever the "flesh" shall be entirely subdued in men, that which " lusteth against the Spirit," will be removed; and there will remain nothing in them warring, either against their own minds, or against the mind of God. With the light of this obvious and certain teaching of the oracles of God, we are prepared to appreciate aright the following remarks of Mr. Finney. In the O. Evan. vol, 2, p. 35, speaking of the sensuality of "ministers themselves," and of the ignorance of many of them, "in regard to the physiology of their own bodies, and of those dietetic principles which are most congenial to bodily health," and of his own past inattention to sensuality, as the great cause of backsliding in himself and others, he says: "I am frequently amazed, that I so far overlooked all those passages, in the Bible, which speak of the influence of the *flesh* upon the mind. The three great enemies of the soul are represented in the Bible, as the world, the flesh, and the devil. I used to preach against the world, and against the devil, and warn Christians against their influence. But I must say, with shame, that I knew but very little of what was meant by those warnings, in the Bible, against the influence of the flesh. Such passages as *these* were not deeply pondered and well considered by me: "*The fleshly mind* [carnal mind] *is enmity against God*" "*To be carnally or fleshly minded is death*." "*If ye live after the flesh ye shall die*." "Therefore mortify your members which are upon the earth." "*He that is Christ's hath crucified the flesh with its lusts*." "I keep under my body, and bring it into subjection" "Be not deceived, God is not mocked; whatsoever a man soweth, that shall he also reap." "*He that soweth to his flesh, shall of the flesh reap corruption*." "*They that are after the flesh do mind the things of the flesh*." These and multitudes of other passages of scripture, I must confess with shame, have been, till recently, very much overlooked by me, i. e. I did not ponder and well understand their meaning. And I can now see that I confounded the influence of the world, and the devil, with that of the flesh. I am now fully convinced, however, that the flesh has more to do with the backsliding of the Church *than either the world or the devil.* Every man has a *body,* and every man's *body,* in this age of the world, is more or less impaired by intemperance of one kind and another."

Now, just view this use of the scripture term "flesh," as a proper *synonyme* of "*intemperance of one kind another,*" pertaining to the body, in connection with the following from the O. Evan. vol. 2, p. 5. Mr. Finney declares: "For myself, I have *very little doubt* that the human constitution is capable of being very nearly, if not entirely renovated or recovered from the evils of intemperance, by a right understanding of, and an adherence to, the laws of life and health. So that, after a few generations, the human body would be *nearly, if not entirely restored to its primitive physical perfection.* If this is so, [and Mr. F. declares, that "*for himself he has very little doubt*" that *it is,*] the time may come, when obedience to the Law of God will imply *as great strength and constancy of affection as Adam was capable of exercising before the fall.*"

The considerate render will perceive, that Mr. Finney evidently resolves "the flesh" into "intemperance of one kind and another,"—into a sort of Dietetic or Physiological Depravity; which "*has more to do*" even "with the backsliding of the Church than either the world or the devil," and that he has "*for himself very little doubt*" that the human constitution is capable of being very nearly, if not entirely renovated or recovered from the evils of intemperance," i. e. of "the flesh," "by a right understanding of, and an adherence to, the laws of life and health. So that, after a few generations, the human body would be nearly, if not entirely *restored to its primitive perfection,*" i. e. such as it possessed "*before the fall.*"

The obvious logical consequences of the foregoing views, we leave the reflecting render to infer for himself. We are aware that the charge of Pelaginnism is often causelessly and slanderously made; but if the system under consideration does not *merit* the epithet Pelagian, we know not to what the term could be properly applied. We are not anxious, however, to identify these sentimens, which Mr. Finney has several times repeated in the O. Evan., with the doctrines of Pelagius. We deem it far more important to contrast them with the facts and principles plainly revealed in God's word. As a most seasonable commentary upon this notion of causing. *by physiological reform,* "the flesh," and of course its "works," to cease, after a few generations, from existence among men, and of restoring the human body to the condition it was in "before the fall," or to its "*primitive physical perfection,*" we suggest Eph. 2: 1—3, "And you hath he quickened, who were dead in trespasses and sins;

wherein in time past ye walked according to the course of this world, according to the prince of the power of the air, the spirit that now worketh in the children of disobedience; among whom also we all had our conversation in times past, in the lusts of our flesh, fulfilling the desires of the flesh and of the mind; and were by nature the children of wrath, even as others." 2 Cor. 5: 14, "For the love of Christ constraineth us; because we thus judge, if one died for all, then were *all dead*." John 3: 3, "Jesus answered and said unto him, Verily, verily, I say unto thee, except a man be born again, he cannot see the kingdom of God." Titus 3: 5, "Not by works of righteousness which we have done, but according to his mercy he saved us, by the washing of regeneration, and renewing of the Holy Ghost." Rom. 5: 12, "Wherefore, as by one man sin entered into the world, and death by sin; and so death passed upon all men, for that all have sinned." 1 Cor. 15: 22, "For as in Adam all die, even so in Christ shall all be made alive."

Will there ever be a time when these truths shall be obsolete?— a period before the resurrection morning when a state of "death in trespasses and sins,"—of " fulfilling the desires of the flesh," shall no longer be the " *natural* " state of man?—when any can see the kingdom of God without being born again, and shall need not the washing of regeneration, nor the *renewing* influence of the Holy Ghost, the antagonist and subduer of the flesh?— when men shall not, " in Adam." be mortal; and death, in the train of sin, shall not " *pass upon all men ?*"—and when there shall be some who will have *no occasion* to " behold," for themselves, "the Lamb of God that taketh away the sin of the world?" If such mighty and *unpromised* results are indeed to be realized, through the mere operation of " physiological reform," we ought neither to smile nor to wonder any more, at the zeal of the Oberlin Professors, concerning Dietetics—concerning " abstinence from meats, *which God hath created to be received with thanksgiving of them which believe and know the truth ;*" nor at their followers' " asking questions for conscience sake," about what they are to eat and drink; nor at their *bodily appliances of any sort*, for verily " *bodily exercise profiteth* " much more than from 1 Tim. 4: 8, we had reason to believe.*

7. *A modified form of the Exercise Scheme.*

We here refer to a scheme of false philosophy, which probably constitutes the basis of their theory of sanctification, or which has, at least, done much to give it its present form.

---

* Let no one suppose that the Temperance cause, in any of its departments, needs the aid of such theorizing. That cause has a far more substantial basis in plain, unperverted declarations of God's word: and it can only suffer loss by becoming associated with speculations so extravagant and unscriptural.

In the O. Evan. vol. 1, p. 41,* it may be seen, that Mr. Finney identifies the *heart, professedly, with the will,* and then, in *fact,* with the *exercises* of the will, i. e. "with volitions or choices," which "control the conduct." *The emotions* or *feelings,* notwithstanding their intimate connection with the will, and their known influence over it, are carefully excluded from his definition of *the heart.* As, according to the scheme, the heart consists in volitions, or choices; and as but *one volition* can be exercised *at once,* the *whole heart,* at any given moment, consists in the *then present volition.* Holiness consists merely in volitions or acts of the will, in which supreme love to God is exercised—sin merely in volitions in which selfishness or supreme self-love is exercised. Mr. Finney expressly denies that any volition or choice is the result of motives *partly* holy and *partly* sinful; and contends repeatedly and zealously, that every volition, or exercise of the will, i. e. of the heart, is either *such precisely* as the Divine Law demands, i. e. is *perfectly holy,* or is *altogether unlike* what the Law demands, i. e. is *entirely sinful.* He predicates sanctification merely of the *acts of the will,* and expressly denies, over and over again, that sanctification works

---

* Mr. Finney says: "By the *heart* I mean the *will.* Emotions, or what are generally termed *feelings,* are often *involuntary* states of mind; i. e. they are not *choices or volitions,* and of course do not *govern the conduct.* Love, in the form of an emotion, may exist in *opposition to the will,* e. g. we may exercise emotions contrary to our conscience and judgment, and in opposition to our will. Thus the sexes often exercise emotions of love towards those to whom all the voluntary powers of their minds feel opposed, and with whom they will not associate. It is true that in most cases the emotions are *with* the will. But they are sometimes, nay often opposed to it. Now it is a *voluntary* state of mind that the Law of God requires. The will controls the conduct: and it is therefore, of course, the love of the heart or *will* that God requires."

Now we doubt not that the Law of God requires *more* than mere desires which are too weak to lead to right action. But leaving this point, we ask, is not the impression likely to be left on not a few minds, by such a paragraph as this, unfavorable to strict views of entire sanctification? Seeing that "it is a *voluntary* state of mind that the Law of God requires," i. e. acts of the will, "*volitions*" "*controlling the conduct,*" and that "emotions or feelings" "are often *involuntary* states," "existing contrary to our conscience and judgment, and in opposition, too, to *our will,* and therefore, on Mr. F's principles, *not coming under the cognizance of Law;*" does it not follow—at least will not many be apt to infer, that *any* feelings, desires or emotions are perfectly consistent with entire sanctification, provided only that there be no act of the will or purpose which shall "*control the conduct?*" But are there not multitudes whose minds swarm daily with polluting thoughts, and who yet have no purpose to gratify their impure desires—perhaps from prudential reasons, a purpose not to do so? And is there not therefore danger, to say the least, that these views, so often repeated and so much insisted upon, will by multitudes be construed into a principle standing in direct opposition to the spirit of the tenth commandment. and of our Saviour's declaration in Matt 5: 28? We would not intimate that Mr. Finney *designs* to teach anything like this, but merely that his zeal to establish a favorite doctrine, has led him unconsciously to adopt and greatly to dwell upon distinctions and principles of *very doubtful tendency,* to say the least, *in relation to the standard of holiness.*

any change in us, so that we become good in ourselves, or that it produces any thing in us, (antecedent to simple, individual, holy exercises,) radical, and abiding, and manifesting itself in right exercises. See e. g. O. Evan. vol. 1, pp. 41, 42.

Such is their exercise scheme. A theory resembling it, had, to a limited extent, been in vogue some time before Mr. Finney embraced these views. But the exercise scheme had been held in connection with the doctrine, that God is the author of all our volitions, holy and unholy, and certain other doctrines fitted, at least, to counteract the legitimate tendency of the scheme to Pelagian Perfectionism.

To this scheme we have space to state, very briefly, only a few even of our prominent objections.

1. Mr. Finney's definition of the heart, making the heart to mean the will, or rather the volitions, is evidently defective. "By the heart," says he, "I mean the will," and from his definition of the heart, he takes care to exclude the feelings or emotions. Now suppose that we substitute the term will for the word heart, in the following passages, where the moral heart is manifestly intended. Ps. 51: 10, 17, "Create in me a clean will, O God;" "A broken and a contrite will, O God, thou wilt not despise." Ps. 81: 12, "So I gave them up to their own will's lust." Mark 10: 5, "And Jesus said unto them, For the hardness of your will, he wrote you this precept;" 16: 14, "Afterward, he appeared unto the eleven as they sat at meat, and upbraided them with their unbelief and hardness of will." Eccl. 9: 3, "Yea, also, the will of the sons of men is full of evil, and madness is in their will, while they live." Prov. 23: 7, "For as he thinketh in his will, so is he." Jer. 17: 9, "The will is deceitful above all things and desperately wicked." Mat. 12: 34, "O generation of vipers! how can ye, being evil, speak good things? For out of the abundance of the will, the mouth speaketh." Ps. 12: 2, "With flattering lips and with a double will do they speak;" 101: 5, Him that hath not a pure will, will I not suffer."

These are only a few, out of a great multitude of passages, which would be made to express nonsense, by such a substitu tion; so that it must be obvious, the term heart includes some things which are not conveyed by the word will, especially when defined as it is by Mr. Finney. For it has been seen that he does not consider the feelings, desires, affections or emotions to be either the will or exercises of the will. So broad a definition of the will, or of the voluntary states, would have made the doctrine of sinless perfection more difficult to be proved. He has taken care, therefore, to cut off his retreat into this comprehensive definition of the will, while attempting to make the heart identical with it. "Emotions," says he, "or what are generally termed feelings, are often involuntary states of mind,

3*

i. e. they are not *choices* or *volitions*, and *of course* do not govern the conduct." Love, in the form of an emotion, may exist in *opposition* to the *will*."—"Thus the sexes often exercise emotions of love towards those to whom *all the voluntary powers* of their minds [i. e. all their *heart*, *if* the *heart* is identical with the *will*] *feel* opposed." * He evidently intends to include in *the heart*, or the exercises of *the heart*, nothing but "choices or volitions, which govern the conduct." Now if emotions of *love* may exist in opposition to the will, so may emotions of *aversion* or of *hatred*. And though he has not said it in so many words, his *principles* here laid down admit directly of the inference, that feelings or emotions of *aversion* towards God, and towards his Law, may exist in opposition to the will—to all the *voluntary powers* of the mind, i. e. to the *whole heart*. So that such feelings or emotions of *aversion* or *hatred* towards God and his Law, would be perfectly *consistent* with a state of *entire sanctification*. His view of the heart, and of what is to be effected by entire sanctification, is evidently unscriptural, and of dangerous tendency. In God's word, *the heart* is not *confined to the will*, i. e. to "*choices* or *volitions* which govern," *immediately*, "the conduct;" but is oftener represented as the fountain, source, or *principle whence* moral *exercises* proceed;" e. g. Prov. 4: 23, "Keep thy heart with all diligence, *for out of it are the issues of life*." Mat. 12: 35, "A good man, *out of* the *good treasure* of *the heart*, bringeth forth *good things;* and an evil man, out of *the evil treasure*, bringeth forth *evil things*." Mark 7: 21, "For from within, *out of the heart of men*, proceed *evil thoughts;*" etc. Now, according to Mr. Finney's philosophy, it is not the *heart* as a *source, fountain,* or *principle*, but its *issues*, that *are to be*, or that *can be sanctified*. "A good man, out of the *good treasure of the heart*, bringeth forth *good things*," says Christ; but Mr. Finney denies that sanctification works any "change *in us*, so that we become *good* in ourselves," and argues that it has respect merely to the *exercises of the will*—to simple, individual *volitions*. According to him, there *is*, there *can be* no cleansing of the *fountain*, but only of the *stream*. But *can* exercises *already* put forth, be *sanctified?*

2d. This *exercise scheme* involves the absurdity, of an alternating series of *regenerations*, and of *total apostasies*, in some who are admitted to be real saints.

According to the theory, a man's character, as holy or unholy, depends, at any given moment, upon his then present exercise of the will. If at any moment his volition is holy, then is he holy in the same degree. But his exercise of the heart, i. e. of *of the will*, is *perfectly* holy, if holy *at all*. Therefore he is at that moment perfectly holy. But if, the next moment, he

* This sort of love, in opposition to the *whole heart*, is something *curious*.

should have an unholy exercise of the will, (and it is admitted that he might,) then, as his volition, i. e. his *whole heart for the time being*, is entirely sinful, *he is entirely sinful.* Thus he may, during the space of a single day, or even of a single hour, be perfectly holy, and then utterly destitute of holiness, and then perfectly holy again. Now at the moment, or during any period while he is exercising a sinful volition, or a succession of sinful volitions, he is not only without anything holy in his *exercises*, but, according to the theory, without any *principle* or *source* remaining *in him*, of holy volitions in future, just as much so, to say the least, as he was previous to his first holy volition; i. e. there is nothing abiding as the result of regeneration, or of any previous operation of the Spirit, which lays the foundation or exists at all *in him*, as a cause or fountain of holy volitions hereafter. And besides, as he transgresses against all the light of his past religious experience, all analogies which can any way apply to a case so hypothetical and monstrous, should lead us to think him more hardened and less likely to exercise a holy volition in future, than he was previous to regeneration, or rather to his first holy volition. Sinning now with his *whole heart*, (i. e. according to the theory,) and without anything *wrought in him* and *abiding*, as the effect of being born of the Spirit; and (as we may suppose) more *awfully guilty* and *hardened* than he was previous to his *first* holy volition, is he not in a condition of apostasy which is *total* while it lasts? But, according to the theory, there is nothing *in him* which *tends* at all to put a period to this condition of *total* sinfulness. Therefore, if he is brought to exercise another holy volition, it must be by a moral change as great and as deserving every way to called a New Birth, as that by which he passed *to* his *first* holy volition *from* the preceding entirely sinful exercise. And the production or causing of the *first* holy volition can with no more propriety be called Regeneration, than the production of *any subsequent* holy exercise, especially of any holy volition immediately following a sinful one. Indeed the theory involves the necessity of a regenerating act for every holy volition; and Mr. Finney says expressly, that Christ produces *no change in us so that we become good in ourselves*, but is himself " *the perpetual Author of all our holy exercises*, and more than intimates that this process must continue not only here, but in the world to come. So that regeneration, *if anything intelligible*, would be, in case of sinlessly perfect Christians, an everlasting new birth, or series of *being born again.* While, in case of imperfect Christians, there must be a series of being born again, alternating with total apostasies. But if this is the correct view of *the thing*, with what propriety can it be called *Regeneration;* i. e. a being born again—a new creation—a resurrection—a passing from death unto life? These figures, which have ever been viewed as es-

ceedingly apposite and striking, certainly lose all their force
and appropriateness, and seem strangely unsuitable, if such is
indeed the idea to which they are applied. What is there in
the thing, if such be the thing, to justify the use of such meta-
phors? The *terms* used to express the thing—the *effects* described in God's word as resulting from the new birth—the new
creation—the spiritual resurrection, or passing from death unto
life, would lead—they *do* lead the plain and judicious reader to
understand nothing less by it, than a *single event* in the history
of the Christian, of *vast moment* and *abiding influence*—an introduction not merely to the exercise of an *individual, holy volition,* but to a new moral state—a mighty and radical change in
his spirit, and temper, and governing purpose of life, produced
by the agency of the Holy Ghost upon his heart, transforming
him into "*a new creature in Christ.*" See e. g. John 1: 13;
Eze. 37: 11—14; Eph. 2: 1; 1 John 3: 14; Rom. 6: 11; Eze.
36: 26; Gal. 6: 15.

The assertion, that the new-creating and transforming agency,
of the Spirit is confined to the simple individual exercises of the
will, and does not work *in us* any permanent *change,* or produce
in us any *abiding principle of holiness, leading to "good works,"*
is contradicted by the letter and spirit of many passages of God's
word already cited, and most evidently by the following: Eph.
2: 10, "For we are his workmanship, *created* in Christ Jesus,
unto good works, which God hath *before* ordained *that we should
walk in them.*" 1 Pet. 1: 23, "Being born again," i. e. having
been regenerated, "not of corruptible seed, but by incorrupti-
ble, by the word of God *which liveth and abideth forever.*"
John 4: 14, "But the water that I shall give him shall be *in him*
a well of water *springing up into everlasting life,*" and of course
never entirely dried up, in any *total* apostasy, *however short.*
5: 24, "Verily, verily, I say unto you, he that heareth my word
and believeth on him that sent me, *hath everlasting life,* and
shall not *come into condemnation,*" i. e. fall from a state of justification through faith in the atoning blood of Christ, "but is
passed from death unto life." Job 17: 9, "The righteous *shall
hold on his way,* and he that hath clean hands shall be *stronger
and stronger.*" 1 John 3: 9. "Whosoever is born of God *doth
not commit sin,*" i. e. *deliberately* and *habitually* as those do,
who have not been born of God, or as persons *would* in a state
of *utter apostasy,* "for his *seed remaineth in him;* and he cannot sin," i. e. as an *apostate* would, "*because he is born* (literally *has been begotten,* regenerated) *of God.*" Upon this passage Pres. Edwards gives the following commentary: "Whosoever is born of God doth not *commit sin,* i. e. he does not
relapse or fall away from righteousness into sin again ["for his
seed remaineth in him,"] i. e. the seed of which he is born of
God, the same seed by which he was begotten of God remaineth.

in him, and therefore he does not fall away to a state and trade
of sin again, out of which he was begotten and born by that
seed." That sound and acute theologian, Andrew Fuller, understood the passage in precisely the same sense: " Whosoever
is born of God doth not *apostatize, for his seed remaineth in
h'm;* and he cannot *apostatize,* because he is born of God."
To these illustrious authorities might be added the opinions of
Macknight, Scott, Doddridge, and a multitude more of pious
and judicious writers, who *substantially* agree in their interpretation of the passage—especially of the phrase, *"for his
seed remaineth in him,"*—all understanding it in a sense
irreconcilable with the supposition that the principle in' Mr.
Finney's exercise scheme, to which we are now adverting,
is true. The phrase, " Whosoever is born of God (i. e. hath
been begotten of God) doth not commit sin," lends no support at
least to *Oberlin* Perfectionism. For if the word "*sin*" here be
made to mean every kind and degree of "*disconformity*" to
God's law, it proves too much for their system: it proves that
every Christian—that *whosoever* has been begotten of God, is
sinlessly perfect from the time of regeneration, onward forever.
For not only is it said, he "doth not commit sin," but "he
cannot commit sin, because he is born of God." According to
this description, there have been no Christians on earth, i. e.
persons sinlessly perfect from the time of regeneration. The
Oberlin Professors themselves do not, so far as we know, believe
that there are, or have been, any such saints on earth, either
under the Old or the New Dispensation; and they *do* believe that
there have been thousands "*who had actually been regenerated
and were real saints,*" to whom this definition of a regenerate
person would not apply. So general and absolute a meaning,
therefore, should not be forced upon the word in this connection;
for it would make the word of God contradict itself. But if we
understand the phrase, "doth not commit sin," in the sense in
which it is interpreted by Edwards, Fuller, and others, i. e. in
the sense to which we are shut up by the exigencies of the passage, it will be fatal to their exercise scheme. They admit that
persons who have been regenerated, do sometimes transgress the
Divine Law—that some real saints are morally imperfect: Not
only so, they contend that when they do sin, they sin with what is
understood to be *their whole heart,* their volitions or choices being *entirely sinful,* and exercised against all the light of previous experience; so that neither in their acts of the will, nor in
themselves, is there any mixture of moral good, or principle of
holiness, any more than there was before they were begotten of
God; and if they ever put forth *another* holy exercise, it must
be the result of another *regeneration.* They must be " created
in Christ Jesus," *again,* "unto good works," or rather unto a
single holy volition, and "pass" anew "from death unto life," i. e.

expressions as imply a comparison of faith as weak or strong,
great or little? Compare Mat. 8: 26; 8: 10; 15: 28; Rom. 4:
19, 20; 14: 1. What is, in this respect, true of faith, is true
also of other " fruit of the Spirit."

4th. This theory of simple exercises is opposed to those texts
which speak of two principles—the flesh, and the spirit, etc.
abiding in regenerate men and lusting or warring against each
other. See e. g. Gal. 5: 17, and Rom. 7: 21—23, with Barnes
in loco.

It is also opposed to those which speak of God's dealings,
arranged to show men their hearts—not their present individual
exercises of the will merely, but the nature or character of the
fountain " out of which are the issues of life." E. g. 2 Chron.
32: 31, " Howbeit, in the business of the ambassadors of the
princes of Babylon, who sent unto him to inquire of the wonder
that was done in the land, God left him to try him, that he might
know all that was in his heart." Deut. 8: 2, "And thou shalt
remember all the way which the Lord thy God led thee these
forty years in the wilderness, to humble thee, and to prove thee,
to know what was in thy heart, whether thou wouldest keep his
commandments, or no." See 2 Ki. 8: 12, 13; 10: 32, 33; also,
Mat. 26: 33, with 26: 74, 75.

It is opposed, also, to those which represent sanctification as
one, continuous, progressive work, begun in God's people, and
persevered in until the day of Jesus Christ, " his seed remaining in them," and so operating that " though (Ps. 37: 24)
they fall, they shall not be utterly cast down," and " when (Mi.
7: 9) they fall, they shall arise." Behold the difference between
repenting David, or repenting Peter, and unregenerate men,
after the commission of similar sins! Prov. 4: 18, " The path
of the just is as the shining light, that shineth more and more
unto the perfect day." Phil. 1: 6, " Being confident of this
very thing, that he which hath begun a good work"—not many
good works—" in you, will perform it until the day of Jesus
Christ."

In short, it must be obvious to every discriminating reader,
that this scheme is inconsistent with any just and scriptural view
of Regeneration, of Sanctification, or of the Saint's Perseverance in Holiness. According to it, we have seen that neither
regeneration nor sanctification relate to the heart, considered as
the seat of the feelings, or as the source of moral exercises, but
merely to the simple, individual acts of the will or volitions—
that regeneration may, with as much propriety, be said to take
place, in case of the thousandth, as of the first holy volition
which the saint puts forth—that a regenerating act is necessary
for every holy exercise—that neither regeneration nor sanctification produces any change in us, or leaves in us any disposition to holiness, tending to secure "good works," and that

therefore, whenever the Christian exercises a sinful volition,
(supposed to be *entirely* sinful,) he is utterly destitute of holiness: for the time, at least, the fountain is dried up, or rather
it sends out nothing but a current of death; and there "remaineth in him" nothing to distinguish him from a person never
regenerated, except (as we might reasonably suppose) increased
hardness of "the heart, or *will;*" so that, if he ever loves God
at all again, it is the result of another "creation in Christ Jesus," unto a holy volition! It may be said, that when God has
produced *one* holy volition in a man, it is his purpose to produce
others, though with apostasies *total* intervening, and finally to
save him. To this we hardly need to reply, that this arrangement, finally, to *save* one, who can in no sense be said to "hold
on his way," is *one thing*—the final *perseverance* of one who
"is born of God," and has "his seed *remaining* in him," is
quite *another thing.* That the scheme involves contradictions to
the teachings of God's word, we trust has been made sufficiently
manifest; and that it must, in connection with so many other
points of kindred influence in the Oberlin system, tend greatly
to promote narrow and shallow views of sanctification, and lead
to self-deception, we have not a shadow of doubt. There is
nothing in the system to counteract, while there is much, very
much to increase its inherent tendency to evil. In this connection, ponder the following doctrine, which occupies a *large space*
in their discussions:

8. *We are Competent Witnesses to our own Entire Sanctification.*

In the O. Evan. vol. 1, p. 44, Mr. Finney remarks: "From
what has been said, you can see the error of those who suppose
we are incompetent witnesses of our own [entire] sanctification."
"So far as we are regarded as honest men, our testimony should
be as satisfactory upon this, as upon any other subject. It is a
point upon which we have the testimony of our own consciousness, which is the highest kind of evidence. And we are just
as competent witnesses to our entire sanctification, as that we
have any religion at all."

Now let us inquire what is implied in being competent to testify
to our own entire sanctification. In doing this, suppose that we
take Mr. Finney's own definitions. *What, then, is implied in
entire sanctification?* At least that every volition, whether
generic or specific, be such every way as to be exactly conformed
to the Law: "Thou shalt love the Lord thy God with all thy
heart, soul, and might, and thy neighbor as thyself," and that
there be no *omission* to choose precisely as this Law, in all of
its diversified applications, and "exceeding broadness" of claim,
demands; not merely that some of the volitions, even though
they be generic or leading ones, but that *all* of them, without

exception, be such *every way* as the Law requires; and that there be no *failure* or *omission* to will and to do according to that "spiritual" and comprehensive rule. Anything short of this would imply defect of sanctification. Even Mr. Finney says, (though not very consistently with some of his principles elsewhere laid down,) that "*partial* sanctification (O. Evan. vol. 1, p. 44) is that state of mind in which it *sometimes* acts selfishly and *sometimes* benevolently." Sanctification evidently cannot be *entire*, unless every volition without a single exception, be such every way as the Divine Law demands.

What is the proper office of *Consciousness*, by the testimony of which Mr. F. says one may know that he is in a state of entire sanctification, or "morally just as perfect as God?"—"I understand consciousness," says he, (O. Evan vol. 1, p. 44,) "to be the mind's *recognition of its own states.*"

What the witness must be able to testify to, then, is all his *voluntary* states, *every* choice or preference which he exercises, and the precise *relation* which every one of his volitions sustains to the Law of God. He must be able to tell from what *governing motive* every volition proceeds, before he can testify concerning its relation to that Law, i. e. before he is prepared to say that the volition exactly meets the claims of the Divine rule. Now, according to Mr. Finney, the power by which he is enabled to *know* that whereof he is to testify, is consciousness, or "the mind's recognition of its own states." Here let us see whether it be true that consciousness alone can enable one to be a competent witness that he is living in a state of entire conformity to the Moral Law.

1. The witness must *recognize* every volition which he puts forth, noting it fully and accurately: and this is as far as, by any natural possibility, he can go by consciousness.

2. Then he must *remember* the precise nature of each of his volitions.

3. Besides, the character of a volition, as holy or sinful, depends upon the governing motive from which it proceeds. "By *motive*," says Pres. Edwards, "I mean the whole of that which moves, excites, or invites the mind to volition." Volition, or willing, considered as a "*state*" of one's mind, *may be* recognized and testified to by consciousness; but the character and claims of Jehovah, "the kingdom of God and his righteousness," or the world with its allurements to sin, not being "states of the mind," i. e. *the mind acting*, cannot be recognized and testified to by consciousness. A man may be *conscious* that he *wills*, but it is improper to say that he is conscious of the *motive* which moves, excites, or invites his mind *to will*. He may be conscious of a "state of mind," but not of that which, as a *motive*, produces or occasions that "state of mind." *

---

* It is not denied that there is a loose and popular use of the word *conscious*

4

4. And then, too, whether a volition be perfectly holy, depends on the *relation* which it sustains to the will of God. Does it exactly meet the demands of this Law? Volition, or willing, is "state of mind;" but the *relation* between an act of the will and the Divine Law, is not *itself* "a state of mind," and therefore cannot be testified to by consciousness. The *comparing* of "a state of mind," with the Divine rule, is not an act of consciousness. In some sense, consciousness is, to the "states of mind." e. g. the exercises *of the will*, what seeing is, to objects of sight: it is that by which they are *noticed*, or *perceived*. Suppose that an architect look at a house—see the several parts of it—and then compare the structure with some rule or order of architecture. The sense of seeing furnishes him with *materials* for the comparison; but it does not itself *compare, infer*, or *decide*. This is evidently the office of a faculty distinct from mere perception. So when a moral agent looks in upon the "states of his mind," and witnesses his volitions, and then *compares* what he observes with the Law of God, consciousness furnishes him with *materials* for the comparison, but does not *itself compare, infer*, or *decide*.

5. But let us inquire whether it be probable that any person so notes and contemplates each of his volitions as to *remember* them all precisely as they are.

Just reflect upon the *rapidity* with which volitions may succeed each other, and the very slight attention which is often given to them. "Thus, in the case of a performer on the harpsichord," says Dugald Stewart, in his Chapter on Attention, "I apprehend that there is an act of the will preceding every motion of every finger, although he may not be able to recollect these volitions afterwards," "the acts of the will being too momentary to leave any impression on the memory." This will serve at least to illustrate the possible and often *actual* rapidity of the volitions, and our exceedingly great liability to forget them. But let it be considered, too, that the difficulty is by no means wholly a natural or intellectual one—that m*mory depends, in no small measure, upon the degree of wakeful and prolonged *attention* given to things—that the *attention* depends upon the *will* and the *affections*—that the acts of the will, especially sinful ones, are a class of facts to which mankind are remarkably *disinclined* to give adequate attention, and of which they are fearfully *prone* to remain, in no slight degree, ignorant. Jer. 17: 9, "*The heart is deceitful above all things, and desperately wicked: who can know it?*" How repeatedly are God's people warned against the *deceitfulness* of the heart—how often have

or *consciousness*, according to which such an expression would be admissible. But this is not the philosophical use of the word, nor s the testimony of *consciousness*, taken in a loose and popular sense, the *highest kind* of evidence—so far from this, that it is often no evidence at all.

the most eminent saints felt and lamented it in their own experience; and how frequent are the cases of self-deception, more or less dangerous and gross, in those who are less spiritual!

Who, we would now ask, who on earth does in fact distinctly *recognize*, and carefully mark every one of his volitions? Who perfectly *remembers* them—not forgetting the *kind* and *degree of intensity* of a single volition? Who, with perfect impartiality and unfailing accuracy, *judges* of all his volitions, unerringly discerning the motive from which each of them proceeds, and knowing exactly the *relation* which they sustain to that Law, the claims of which "are exceeding broad?" In short, who is a *competent* witness to his *own entire sanctification?* The question, it will be perceived, is not whether the testimony of consciousness, so far as it goes, can be relied on; but whether any person on earth can reasonably be supposed, as a matter of fact, so carefully to *recognize*—so fully and exactly to *remember*—and with such unbiased and unerring judgment to *compare* his volitions with the Law of God, as to know that he is in a state of entire sanctification? And here let it be observed, that, in the discussion of this point, we have taken the narrowest view of sanctification, in order to conform to Mr. Finney's own definitions; predicating sanctification, not of the "fountain" of moral exercises, but simply of the "stream"—some would say, of a *part* only even of that—of the volitions, or mere acts of the will after excluding the *feelings*. But, on Mr. Finney's own principles, this doctrine of competency to testify to one's own entire sanctification, is embarrassed with several difficulties not yet mentioned. We have space to state only the following:

He says: "*Partial* sanctification is that state of mind in which it *sometimes* acts selfishly, and *sometimes* benevolently," i. e. (as he explains it) a state of mind in which it sometimes exercises *entirely sinful* volitions, and sometimes *entirely holy* volitions If such be *partial* sanctification, how *many* entirely holy volitions must be exercised in uninterrupted succession before the sanctification is *entire?* As, according to him, sanctification produces *no change in us*, but relates merely to the volitions exercised, and as an occasional *interruption* of the succession of holy exercises by sinful ones causes sanctification to be "*partial*," or proves it to be not *entire*, it is of no small importance that the witness know how long exactly he must continue his series of perfectly holy volitions in order to testify credibly to his being in a state of *entire* sanctification. Now as the Bible had nothing to do with the getting up of this theory, we shall look in vain to that for a solution of *its difficulties*. For ourselves, therefore, we leave it to any one who may be desirous of testifying to his own sinless perfection, to settle for himself this "boundary question" between *partial* and *entire* sanctification. But Mr. Finney argues that if a person cannot know that he is entirely sanctified, he cannot (by the same rule) know that he is *not.* At this we marvel. Consider for a moment the nature of the case. If a person should discover that one, only *one,* of his volitions or moral exercises, in a week—may we say in a *month?*—on an average, is sinful, he would know that he is *not* entirely sanctified. While, *if* he were carefully to note, perfectly to remember, and accurately to compare a *thousand* volitions, with the claims of God's Law, during each month, there might be others not so carefully noted, not so perfectly remembered, not so accurately compared. There is, therefore, so to speak, an almost infinite difference between knowing that we are, and knowing that we are not entirely sanctified; and this, too, on Mr. Finney's own principles of sanctification. There is an immense disparity in *the amount of facts* necessary to be known in the two cases. But this is not all. With an equal number of moral exercises to be known, there would be an incomparably greater *moral* liability to err by judging too favorably, than too unfavorably of ourselves. While the Bible abounds with exhortations against thinking "more highly of ourselves than we ought to think," no instance is recollected in which God's people, however self-abased, are warned against entertaining too mean and humble a view of their own spiritual attainments.

Mr. Finney asserts, too, that "we are just as competent witnesses to our *entire* sanctification, as that we have any religion at all." To this mere assertion, it is quite sufficient to reply, that, on his own principles of sanctification, a person might far more reasonably be supposed to know that *some* of his moral exercises are holy, than that *all* of them, without exception, perfectly meet the demands of the Law of God; and of course might testify far more *credibly* that *some* of his volitions are holy, than that *all* of them are so—that he *sometimes* wills right, than that he *never fails to will precisely as the Moral Law requires.* Is not the difference great enough to be discerned by the dullest intellect, between even an "infallible assurance *of faith,*" "of being in a state of grace,"—an assurance "founded upon the Divine truth of the promises of salvation, the inward evidence of those graces unto which these promises are made, the testimony of the Spirit of adoption witnessing with our spirits that we are the children of God,"—and knowing that we are in a state of sinless perfection—in a state in which we *never* fail to will, to choose, or to prefer exactly *every way,* as the Divine Law, in all its spirituality and broadness of claim, requires? Many are believed (as the result of diligent study of God's word, and of lives of holy effort and self-denial, and of prayerful scrutiny of their feelings and their conduct, in the diversified circumstances of varied trial) to have attained to the former, who have expressly disclaimed attainment to the latter.

This doctrine of competency, resulting directly from mere consciousness, to testify to our own entire sanctification, and this stress laid upon the giving of such testimony, are as unscriptural as they are unphilosophical; and obviously tend to open wide a door for the coming in of delusion—of a spirit of egotism—of self-righteousness, and of carnal security, undisturbed by due self-distrust and wakeful self-examination—and of denouncing such as are unwilling to *testify to like personal attainments.*

It is true, that God urges his people to *examine* themselves. But this implies their proneness to self-ignorance; their liability to self-deception; their lack, in a degree at least, of self-knowledge; and is surely not inconsistent with what he says directly of the deceitfulness of the heart, and of the folly of trusting in it; and with his explicit warnings against confiding in the testimony which they *receive* from consciousness as being sufficiently *full,* sufficiently *remembered,* and *compared faithfully enough* with the Divine rule, to enable them, at once, as it were by intuition and with perfect *certainty,* to know that they are "as free from all sin as was the Lord Jesus Christ," or "morally just as perfect as God." Although the apostle Paul enjoins often the most scrutinizing *self-examination,* (1 Cor. 14: 31; 2 Cor. 13: 5,) yet he condemns expressly the idea of deciding, from the *absence* of testimony of consciousness against us, that we are in a state of entire conformity to the Divine Law. 1 Cor. 4: 3—5, " But with me it is a very small thing that I should be judged of you, or of man's judgment: *yea, I judge not mine own self; for I know nothing by myself,* [although I am not conscious to myself of anything wrong or criminal,] *yet am I not hereby justified: but he that judgeth me is the Lord—therefore judge nothing before the time,"* etc. The pious and judicious Doddridge paraphrases the passage thus:

" Nor indeed do I so *judge myself,* as if my case were finally to be determined by my own apprehensions concerning it. *For* though I bless God I am not *conscious* to myself of anything criminal, of any *designed* neglect of my office, or unfaithfulness in my trust, *yet I am not hereby justified:* that is not the main thing in question; I know *partiality to ourselves* may often lead us to *overlook* many faults for which God may another day condemn us. But he that *judgeth me,* the Person by whose judgment I am to stand or fall, is the Lord Jesus Christ, who *searcheth the hearts and trieth the reins* of the children of men. Therefore be strictly careful that *ye judge nothing before the appointed time,* i. e. until he, the great Lord of all, shall come, who 'shall bring to light the *hidden things of darkness,* and shall manifest *all the secret counsels of the hearts.*'" See Barnes' excellent note upon this passage, or Macknight's, or, if you please, Adam Clarke's.

4*

"God is greater than our heart, and knoweth all things."
When we see enough in ourselves to condemn us, much more
does God. When we are not conscious of wrong intentions,
and are truly sincere, then indeed (trusting in Christ) "have
we confidence toward God," so that wo can come "boldly (not
before our fellow men, to testify to our own entire sanctification, but) unto the throne of grace to obtain mercy and find
grace to help in time of need." The confidence, at such times,
is not knowledge through the direct and certain evidence
of consciousness, that we are in a state of sinless perfection,
but confidence by which we may say: "If any man sin, we have
an Advocate with the Father, Jesus Christ the Righteous."
The following passages deserve to be pondered by those who
are fondly trusting to consciousness,———as furnishing sufficient evidence of sinless perfection. Prov. 16: 25, "There
is a way that seemeth right unto a man; but the end thereof are
the ways of death." Prov. 28: 26, "He that trusteth in his own
heart is a fool." Acts 26: 9, "I verily thought with myself
that I ought to do many things contrary to the name of Jesus of
Nazareth."

The truth is, he who testifies to his own entire sanctification,
assumes an "unseemly" responsibility. The Christian should
indeed be a "witness for Christ," by the "light" of a blameless example "before men;" and by laying down his life, if
need be, in attestation of his love to the Saviour, and of his
confidence in God. He may, when wrongfully accused, assert
sometimes, as Paul did, the sincerity of his aims, and refer to
his course of life for proof. And he should "be ready always
to give an answer to every man that asketh him a reason of the
hope that is in him, with meekness and fear." But how different from all this, is the practice of testifying before men to one's
own entire sanctification! Who is competent to give such testimony? Can the giving of such testimony—conflicting as it
does most manifestly with scripture and correct mental philosophy—tend to honor God? Honor to the Saviour is the pretence
for thus testifying. But when or where was the Saviour ever
honored, or the spirit of genuine, humble piety promoted by this
practice? The evil tendency of it—especially where great stress
is laid upon it, and where the doctrine of competency to testify
to one's own sinlessness, on the ground of the mere testimony
of consciousness, is often and zealously inculcated—is abundantly evident from the very nature of things; and has been
illustrated more than once by painful facts.* Nor is there any
reason to expect that its tendency to foster self-conceit, spiritual
pride, and delusion, will be counteracted either by any doctrines
with which it may be connected, in the Oberlin system, or by

* Mr. Mahan, on p. 196 of his Book, says: "It is in giving such testimony
that we are chiefly to glorify Christ and benefit our fellow men."

Mr. Finney's mode of exhibiting the nature and office of consciousness. In this connection, we may perhaps be permitted to remark, that Mr. F's views of the office of consciousness are not characterized by an unusual degree of *precision*. Although he defines consciousness to be "the mind's recognition of *its own states*," he asks: "How do I know that I *breathe*, or love, or hate, or *sit*, or *stand*, or *lie down*, or *rise up?*" etc. "I answer: by my own consciousness." (See O. Evan, vol. 2, p. 50.) Now, are we to understand, that the *corporeal* exercises and positions of "*breathing, sitting, standing, lying down*, and *rising up*," are "states of the mind," and as such recognized by *consciousness?* It is only the testimony of consciousness *strictly* so called, and acting in its proper sphere, and actually noting the exercises, or states of the mind, that is regarded by real philosophers as "the highest kind of evidence." And we have proved that this testimony *does not and cannot extend to all* that must be known to enable a person to testify to his own sinless perfection.

But if we are not competent to testify to our *own* entire sanctification, are we to the entire sanctification of *others?* We are indeed commanded "not to believe every spirit, (i. e. every teacher who pretends to be inspired by the Spirit of God,) but to *try* the spirits (i. e. the spiritual pretensions of such teachers), whether they be from God; because many *false* prophets are gone forth into the world,"—to *try* them by comparing their doctrine and conduct with the *word of God*. And our Saviour, speaking of false prophets, declared that their *unholy conduct* would be evidence of the falsehood of their pretensions. "Ye *shall know them* [to be hypocrites] *by their fruits.*" But who can, without the most unwarrantable presumption, "judge before the time," so as to decide that any one of Adam's race is sinlessly perfect? Who is competent to affirm, that the desires, volitions and thoughts of his most intimate acquaintances are at every moment, during hours, days, months and years, without interruption or failure, just such *every way* as the Law of God requires? What human being is fully qualified to share with the Omniscient, the distinctive title of "*the Searcher of hearts?*" The conclusion is inevitable, therefore, *that without a direct revelation from Heaven, the entire sanctification of no person on earth could be proved, even if it were attained.*

9. *Further Illustrations of their Yielding to the Temptation, and Logical Necessity of their False Position.*

1. The frequency with which Mr. Finney, Mr. Mahan, and others under the influence of their system, speak complainingly of "a legal spirit," of "legal sermons," of "legal preachers," and of "legal Christians," living "under legal bondage."

2. Their *constant use*, and *literal application* of the phrases:

Take God at his word. Believe that he means just what he says. And this will *at once* bring you into the state of mind after which you inquire." In the O. Evan. vol. 2, p. 57, he teaches in like manner the doctrine of instantaneous sanctification by faith. Mr. Mahan, on p. 161 of his Book, after describing the Redeemer, says: " Now let me ask you, reader, do you believe with all your heart," "that Christ has provided a redemption *for you*—a redemption so perfectly and specifically adapted to your particular case, that you can now go to him and be cleansed from all that is impure and unholy, and so transformed into his likeness that your *entire character* shall hereafter present a *pure reflection of his image?*" " Do you believe that you may bring to him your *temper*, your *appetites*, your *propensities*, your *entire habits*, and have them *all* brought into sweet subjection to the will of God?" Much more to the same effect might be quoted. This doctrine is nearly allied, in its nature, to the one last mentioned, and is attended with a similar difficulty. It is not only unscriptural, but manifestly absurd. To be sanctified through *faith*, (as they understand its nature and offices,) is to be sanctified or become *perfect*, through *perfection* in holiness. According to one part of their system, as we have seen, holiness consists merely in exercises of the heart, i. e. of *the will;* and every exercise which is holy in *any* degree, is perfectly holy, i. e. all *every way* that God, in view of one's capacity and knowledge, does or can *require*. Not only so, but in the O. Evan. vol. 1, p. 138, Mr. Finney declares one element of faith to be " that confidence of the *heart* that yields *all* our *voluntary powers* up to the *control of truth.*" i. e. in the *very exercise of faith* there is " a yielding up of *all* one's voluntary powers" (or of *all* to which the work of sanctification has respect) to "*the control of truth.*" It is not easy to see wherein "yielding up all one's voluntary powers to the control of truth," falls at all short of Mr. F's own repeated definitions of entire sanctification. It is all that the Law of God requires, himself being judge. It implies *perfection* in holiness, according to his own principles.

Mr. Mahan, too, on p. 110 of his Book, in showing what is requisite in order *to receive* the blessings of entire sanctification, or of the New Covenant, mentions among other things, " an actual reception of Christ, and reliance upon him for all those blessings in all their fulness—*a surrender of your whole being to him,* that he may accomplish in you all the 'exceeding great and precious promises' of the New Covenant." But according to one of his own definitions of Christian perfection, this *prerequisite* implies the *present* possession of the very thing to be *attained.* On p. 10 he says, (where his avowed object is to give a correct definition of perfection in holiness:) " In the Christian, perfection in holiness implies *the consecration of his whole being* to Christ—the subjection of all his powers and susceptibilities to the control of one principle. 'faith on the Son of God.' "This is what the Moral Law demands of him in his circumstances."

Besides, we have his own declaration, made in the form of a prominent argument, for the attainableness [or attainment] of perfect holiness in this life, that very many promises of the Bible are *conditioned* on this state, i. e. that we must be *perfectly* holy in order *to have* these numerous and important promises *fulfilled* to us. On p. 43, he says: "I infer that perfect holiness is attainable in this life, from the *many promises* of Scripture which are *conditioned on this state*," i. e. *a state of perfection.* We must therefore go to Christ. perfect *already*, as the condition or *sine qua non* of having "all the 'exceeding great and precious promises of the New Covenant," "accomplished in us." The New Covenant (as he understands it) includes *all* promised blessings—"a continued state of pure and perfect holiness"—"pardon of all sin"—"the perpetual fruition of the Divine presence and favor"—and "the general spread of the gospel among mankind." There can be no promises of importance to us. the blessings of which are not included in the New Covenant. His argument, then, from *promises* being *conditioned* on a state of *perfect* holiness, is without any conceivable force, unless we suppose that perfection in holiness is a *prerequisite* to receiving the fulfilment of the New Covenant. Is not the attainment of perfection in holiness, then, conditioned on *previous* perfection in holiness—on being *already* what we seek *to be?* Can there be any logical escape from this conclusion, on the principles which Mr Finney and Mr. Mahan have repeatedly advanced in relation to the *conditions* of sanctification? Let it be distinctly noted, then, that according to the principles of "Oberlin Perfectionism," entire sanctification is *conditioned* on *previous* perfection. To *become* sinlessly perfect, you must go to the Saviour *already perfect.* And is this. we ask, a doctrine fitted to exalt Christ? Does all that they say about "the *whole gospel*," "*full* salvation," "*complete* redemption." and "a *perfect* Saviour." dwindle, as to its *real grace* and *efficacy*, to this less than orthodox idea, "*First* be thou *perfect: come thus* unto me, and *then* will I *keep* thee, *as thou art—perfect?*" * Nothing

* The *grace* of the system is reduced even below this less than evangelical standard, by those who teach that persons, after receiving the New Covenant by *perfect faith*, fall again into sin. Even after going to the Saviour *perfect,* they are not *kept* so by him!
The ground which seems of late to be taken, is that permanent. entire sanctification is conditioned on *perfect faith continued.* That is, persons may *become* perfectly and perpetually holy, *if* they will *only* go to Christ. exercising that *perfect* faith which works by *perfect* love, *perfectly* purifies the heart. and *perfectly* overcomes the world—implying "a surrender of their *whole being* to Christ," or "a yielding up of all their *voluntary powers* to the *control of truth*," (and of course to the control of the Moral Law, which is

exalts Christ *really* so much as the unvarnished, simple truth of the gospel, as it was understood by Baxter, Edwards, Whitefield, Brainerd, Fuller, and Payson. All strained, theoretical lauding results in real detraction from the glory of his grace. In this system, the chief glory is in reality given to him who goes, *perfect in holiness* to Christ; or rather, entire sanctification is so *conditioned* as to make its actual attainment morally impossible. The difficulty is easily stated and obvious. You cannot be *wholly sanctified*, until you exercise *perfect faith*. But you cannot exercise the *perfect faith* described as the *prerequisite*, without being *already* wholly sanctified. The condition includes the very thing to be obtained on that condition. *To be perfect*, is the condition on which you are, through the wonderfully rich and efficacious " provisions of the gospel," *to become perfect!*

12. *Sufficiency of Gospel Provisions to Secure our Entire Sanctification in the Progress of the Present Life.—But in what sense sufficient?*

On p. 22 of his Book, Mr. Mahan declares: "The question whether entire perfection in holiness is attainable [attained] in this life, depends *exclusively* upon the question, what are the nature and extent of the provisions of the gospel for our present sanctification, and of the 'exceeding great and precious promises' of divine grace? In pursuing our inquiries in respect to this question, we are to look away from our condition and circumstances as sinners, and from our natural powers as moral agents, to the provisions and promises of the grace of God."

Here and elsewhere it is conceded by Mr. Mahan, that the mere possession of *natural* powers as moral agents, adequate to keep perfectly the Divine Law, proves nothing at all in respect to *actual* perfection in holiness—that the question depends *exclusively* on "the nature and extent of the provisions of the gospel for our present sanctification." He therefore dwells much upon the glorious nature and extent of the provisions of the gospel, endeavoring to demonstrate their *sufficiency* to consummate, in the progress of this life, the work of entire sanctification. The *sufficiency* of the provisions of Divine grace for *this purpose*, is evidently viewed by him, and all the advocates of the system, as their stronghold. It is here that many have been deceived, taking that for proof which either proves nothing, or proves too much for their theory. In what sense, then, are the provisions of the gospel *sufficient?* Is it meant that they are *efficacious,*

included in the truth,) *if* they will *only do this*, and continue to do *it*, without any interruption or short coming! In other words, persons will become permanently and perfectly conformed to the Law of God, *if* they shall in fact permanently and perfectly conform to the Law of God; that is, permanent, entire sanctification is *conditioned* (according to this view) *on itself?* You shall be perfect as long as you shall continue to be perfect!

effectual, so as *actually* to overcome every obstacle to holiness of life; e. g. unbelief, disinclination, hardness of heart, blindness of mind, all selfishness, and in fact to *secure* or certainly bring about the object, viz. entire sanctification? Are they of such a nature, and such an extent as to *secure* perfect faith—perfect love—in short, entire sanctification? Do they effectually produce compliance with the *conditions* of entire sanctification, and lead *in fact* to the consummation—perfection in holiness? If they could be proved to be, in *this* sense, sufficient, the argument from their *sufficiency* would indeed be conclusive. But it would prove too much for those who use it. It would prove, at least, that *all* who are "real saints," are entirely sanctified. For, according to Mr. Mahan's view of "particular redemption,"— a redemption specifically adapted to the *particular case of every Christian*—the "sufficient" gospel provisions are sufficient in precisely the same degree for *one*, that they are for any *other*. If, then, "the question of entire perfection in holiness depends (as he says) *exclusively*" on the nature and extent of the provisions of Divine grace; and if these provisions are (as he says) specifically adapted to the *peculiarities of each particular case*, then what these provisions accomplish in *one* Christian, they may be expected to accomplish in *every other*. Do the "sufficient provisions" banish the unbelief, remove *all* the evil propensities and wrong habits, and effect the entire sanctification of *one* Christian? Then, being equally adapted to do this for every *other*, they are effectual. at once—not progressively—for the entire sanctification of *all* "real saints." But this is more than either Mr Mahan or Mr. Finney believes. In this sense of sufficiency, therefore, the argument must be abandoned, unless they so alter their theory as to assert that *all Christians* are thus sanctified; or, in other words, that there are *no* "real saints," but those who are at once wholly sanctified as soon as they are regenerated.

But if, by "*sufficiency* of gospel provisions," it be meant merely that they are such, that. *if* believers were actually to exercise "that confidence of the heart that yields *all their voluntary powers* up to the control of *truth*," or were, with *all* the faith which God does or can require, to "*surrender their whole being to Christ*, that he might" *thus* "accomplish in them all the 'exceeding great and precious promises' of the New Covenant"— if it be meant merely, that *if* Christians were, in fact, to use *all* the provisions of the gospel precisely as they *ought* to use them, then might they be entirely sanctified—it is easy to see that the argument proves absolutely nothing in respect to *actual* entire sanctification. For the very question in debate is: Do any, *in fact*, so appreciate all the motives to holiness—so use all the rich provisions of the gospel, as to be instantaneously and entirely sanctified in the "progress of this life?"

5

There is a sense in which we may say that the sanctions of the Law, eternal life and eternal death, are a sufficient motive to obedience, i. e. sufficient, if duly appreciated. In view of right reason, they infinitely outweigh any motives to sin. But do men, *in fact*, duly appreciate these motives to obedience? And are any, by an *actual* right use of these (absolutely, not relatively) mighty motives, sinless? To say that men *do* actually obey perfectly, because, in the sanctions of the Law, God has given *sufficient* reasons (in themselves considered) for such obedience, is manifestly illogical and contradictory to known facts. So, too, to say that some *do*—with perfect faith—with ac-*tual "surrender of their whole being to Christ,"* and of "all their voluntary powers to the control of truth"—*appropriate* and *use* the provisions of the gospel, and thus become sinless, because these provisions *would be* sufficient for their entire sanctifica-tion, *if* thus perfectly appropriated and used, is taking for granted the very thing to be *proved*. Though Jehovah could in truth ask (Is. 5: 4): "*What could have been done more to my vineyard that I have not done in it?*" yet an abuse of his mer-*cies* justified the rebuke, "*wherefore, when I looked that it should bring forth grapes, brought it forth wild grapes?*" All this is relevant to prove men's obligation—increased obligation—but most manifestly it proves nothing in favor of the doctrine of their *actual* perfect obedience? It is remarkable, that though Mr. Finney and Mr. Mahan regard the question of entire sanc-tification, as depending *exclusively* on the nature and extent of the provisions of the gospel, the former has devoted one whole Lecture, or No. of a Lecture, to show whence it is that these very provisions *fail* to produce entire sanctification. (See O. Evan. vol. I p. 121—) And it would appear, from his own show-ing, that through men's voluntary ignorance and unbelief, these "sufficient" gospel provisions have, at least in the vast majority of cases, been *unproductive* of that for which they are "suffi-cient," i. e. of entire sanctification. Is not the attempt, then, to prove sinless perfection in this life, from the nature and extent of those provisions, utterly futile? Has it not proved an entire failure? For if the provisions of the gospel do not banish *un-belief and voluntary ignorance*—if they do not *effectually* work in men to believe, to love, and spiritually to know the things of Christ—if, as Messrs. Finney and Mahan contend, they may be rejected by unbelief, and are *conditioned* on a sort of faith imply-ing *present* perfection—a condition not likely to be complied with—a condition *including* the very blessing *to be obtained*—how does the mere existence of such provisions prove anything, one way or the other, in respect to *actual* entire sanctification? Besides, in *this view* of the provisions of the gospel, it is obvious that the question of the actual attainment of perfection in holi-ness, does not depend "*exclusively*" nor even *mainly* upon those "*provisions;*" but upon *our exercising perfect faith.* But faith, as has already been remarked, works by *love, purifies the heart,* and *overcomes the world.* Acts 15: 9; Gal. 5: 6; 1 John 5: 4. *Perfect* faith therefore works by *perfect love*—*perfectly* purifies the heart—*perfectly* overcomes the world. *Perfect* faith implies the *perfection* of the other Christian graces. According to their own view of what is included in faith, it implies *present perfection in holiness.* How palpably absurd then to say! "Behold the sufficiency of the provisions of the gospel for our present entire sanctification!" They are *such* that one has *only to go to Christ with perfect faith,* i. e. only to *go already perfect,* and then entire sanctification, or perfection in holiness, is at once the *result!*" So that sanctification, on this plan, turns out to be sanctification resulting from previous perfection in holiness—and the entirely sanctified make themselves *to differ* from others by their own exercise of *perfect* faith. And those who "testify" to their own *entire* sanctification, *may* testify quite as much to the *praise* of their own *perfect* faith, as to the glory of the grace of Christ. One *might* say: "On such a day I went with perfect faith—with 'all my voluntary powers yielded up to the control of truth'—with my 'whole being surrendered to Christ'—with my *heart purified,* and the *world under my feet*—to the Son of God; and then, through the riches of his grace, I *became* (in proportion to my knowledge and capacity) just as holy as *I was before!*" Alas, how little additional glory is the Saviour likely to receive by this theory, as "a *perfect* Redeemer," and as "the Author of a *full* salvation," etc.! Indeed, if the gospel provisions are only, in *such a sense,* sufficient for our entire sanctification in "the progress of this life," and are *thus* conditioned, is it not absolutely amazing that any—much more that men of *logical* minds—should attempt to draw thence an argument—their favorite and strongest argument—for the doctrine of *sinless perfection attained?*

But Mr. Finney argues, that if nothing can be proved from these *conditionally* sufficient provisions of the gospel, in regard to actual entire sanctification, then we cannot prove that any will be *actually* saved, seeing that salvation is conditioned on repentance and faith, or on obedience to the gospel. At this, too, we marvel. If God's "*effectual calling*" of sinners to repentance, to faith, to holiness, and *thus* to salvation, were *conditioned* on their *previously* repenting—believing—obeying, then the argument would have some force. But it was God's promise in the Covenant of Redemption, his purpose from eternity—not with an *if*—*effectually* to call, to justify, and finally to glorify those who were ordained to eternal life; and as soon shall his throne pass away, as one jot or one tittle of his revealed promise or purpose fail of fulfilment. See e. g. Is. 53: 10—12; 2 Tim. 1: 9; Acts 13: 48; Rom. 8: 28—30. Let Mr. F. prove that it is, in the same sense, God's purpose entirely, and *at once* to sanctify Christians, individually, by leading them to *comply with the conditions* of sanctification—that it is to save them by *"effectually calling"* them to repentance, to faith, to "the path of the just which is as the shining light that shineth more and more unto the perfect day." and thus to the world of "just men made perfect;"—let him prove this; and those Perfectionists who believe that there *are* no "real saints," but the *entirely* sanctified, will thank him for performing the difficult task, and for overturning, at least, a part of his own creed. For this would prove that all *Christians* are thus sanctified. But unless this point can be made out, his argument is based upon a false analogy; and the attempt to prove *actual* entire sanctification, from the *conditionally* "sufficient provisions of the gospel," manifestly results in a total failure.

13. *Arguments which Prove Too Much, if they Prove Anything.*

One striking indication of the unsoundness of "Oberlin Perfectionism," is that all the arguments which have been, or can be adduced in its favor, either prove nothing to the purpose, or prove too much. Of some of these, we have already taken a passing notice; but there are many more; some of the most plausible of which we will now briefly examine.

1. *Imperfect justification,* or *else there are no Christians except the entirely sanctified.*

Mr. Mahan, in attempting to prove that one great object to be accomplished, as the result of Christ's death, is the attainment of perfection in holiness in *this life,* quotes Rom. 8: 3, 4, and endeavors to show that the phrase, "righteousness of the Law," "means the precepts of the Law, or the moral rectitude which the Law requires." But says he: "If *justification* were the thing primarily referred to in this phrase, still the moral rectitude required by the Law, i. e. *sanctification*, is implied in it. For if Christ should *justify,* and not to *the same extent sanctify* his people, he would save them *in,* and not *from* their sins. "The phrase 'righteousness of the Law,' then, directly and primarily means or obviously implies the precepts of the Law, or the moral rectitude required by the Law. To have this righteousness fulfilled in us, implies that it be *perfectly accomplished in us,* or that we are brought into *perfect conformity* to the moral rectitude required by the Law. This is declared to be *one of the great objects of Christ's death.*" [i. e. to bring Christians—his people—"into perfect conformity," in the progress of this life, "to the moral rectitude required by the Law."] See Mahan's Book, p. 27. In relation to this argument we remark,

(1.) That if a leading object or purpose of Christ's death was to secure the entire sanctification of Christians during the progress of this life, then either all Christians are thus sanctified, or an important object or purpose of the Omniscient in his death has failed. What Paul says in Rom. 8: 3, 4, is true of all (Rom. 8:1) who are in a state of *justification*—who are in Christ Jesus. If it was "one of the great objects of Christ's death," to bring Christians—all Christians, into a state of "perfect conformity to the moral rectitude required by the Law, and this, too, as soon as they come into a state of justification; then either all "who are in Christ Jesus," are *entirely* sanctified; or, just so far as there are any Christians not so sanctified, "one great object of Christ's death" has failed. Infidels will thank Mr. M. for such an interpretation of the Bible as will make it appear that the gates (or the counsels) of hell have so triumphantly prevailed against one great object of Christ's kingdom for eighteen centuries, that what Christ *meant* to accomplish in all his people, has failed to be fulfilled in "thousands" of real saints, on account of "their ignorance and unbelief." But we remark,

(2.) That if the "one great object of Christ's death," was merely so to provide for the present, instantaneous, entire sanctification of his people, that *if* they would actually put away *all* unbelief, and come to him with perfect faith, with their "*whole being* surrendered to him," and "all their voluntary powers yielded up to the control of *truth*," then might they have "the righteousness of the Law" fulfilled in them—it proves, as we have abundantly shown, absolutely nothing. For it might be said of every sinner in the universe: *If* he should put away *all* unbelief—if he should exercise that "confidence of the heart" towards God, "that yields up all his voluntary powers to the control of truth," and "surrender his *whole being* to his Creator" in "perfect faith," he would then be in a state of perfect conformity to the Moral Law, at least according to Mr. Mahan and Mr. Finney's definitions of such a state. All this "arguing proves" just about as much as to say: "*If* people would only be perfect, they would *be perfect*." We remark,

(3.) That Mr. Mahan's reasoning in respect to justification deserves especial notice. He declares that "the moral rectitude required by the Law, i. e. sanctification, is implied in justification. For if Christ should *justify*, and not to the *same extent* to sanctify his people, he would save them *in*, and not *from* their sins." Now this has no relevancy to the purpose of his argument, and is utterly impertinent in the connection in which it stands, if it does not mean that *entire* justification *so implies* *entire* sanctification, that a person is not wholly pardoned until

---

* Mr. Finney declares repeatedly that *unbelief* is the foundation or source of *all* sin. If it is so, then he who puts away *all* unbelief, or *all that* from which sin proceeds, becomes thenceforth sinlessly perfect.

he attains to a state of "perfect conformity to the moral rectitude required by the Law." He could not have intended to say that justification implies a *beginning* of the work of sanctification, to be "performed (Phil. 1: 6) until the day of Jesus Christ," or merely that when God, the *first moment* that a repenting sinner casts a look of confidence to Christ, *fully* justifies or forgives him, he does it with the purpose to carry on the work of his grace, *begun* in repentance, and to make it *ultimately* as complete as justification; so that the penitent, *at first* freely and fully forgiven, shall be *quite as fully* washed and sanctified *before* his admission into Heaven. This, though true, would have been not only irrelevant, but fatal to the purpose of his argument. If he meant anything suited to the wants of his argument, it must have been, that *complete* justification and *entire* sanctification are *simultaneous*—that justification is not complete, until sanctification is *entire*. Here let it be observed, that imperfect justification—incomplete forgiveness—is no justification at all. One sin unforgiven would as *certainly* sink the soul to hell, as ten thousand. No one, then, could be in Christ, an heir of life eternal, having his sins forgiven, unless he were entirely sanctified. Only the sinlessly perfect could say:— "Wherefore, being *justified* by faith, we have *peace* with God, through our Lord Jesus Christ." Of none but the entirely sanctified could it be said: "There is therefore now *no condemnation* to them." What should we say, then, of the case of Abraham, "the father of the faithful?" "He received not that measure of the Holy Spirit, which produces the entire sanctification of the soul." So contends Mr. Finney. Either, then, he was entirely sanctified, without the aid of the Holy Spirit, or he was not so justified but that the wrath of God continued to *abide upon him!* Yet says an apostle, (Jas. 2: 23,) "And the scripture was fulfilled which saith, Abraham believed God, and it was imputed unto him for righteousness, (justification,) and he was called the Friend of God."

Is this doctrine of imperfect, progressive justification, or of complete justification, *simultaneous* with entire sanctification, any part of the Christianity of the Bible?—Yet we would not mention this doctrine as *new;* or as *peculiar* to "Oberlin Perfectionism." It prevailed extensively before the days of Luther. A favorite it has long been with the Mother of Harlots. According to her, if Christians "work more and more, grace doth more *increase*, and they are *more and more justified*." See Bishop McIlvaine, on Justification, p. 23. This is not the first time since the days of Luther, that "reformation," so called, has been only a new edition of old errors. We do not charge Mr. M. with intending this revival of a false doctrine, but simply with using an argument to establish his theory which necessarily includes this. The meaning of his very explicit declaration, above quoted, harmonizes with some other parts of this book—for example, with what he says on p. 123: "We are now prepared for a distinct contemplation of the *grand mistake* into which the *great mass* of Christians appear to have fallen, in respect to the gospel of Christ. It is this: expecting to obtain *justification*, and not at the *same time*, and to the *same extent*, *sanctification* by *faith in Christ*."—If the provisions of Divine grace, which secure the conversion of the soul, are arranged and specifically adapted to secure entire sanctification at the *same time* with *entire* justification; if this is in fact the *purpose*— the *plan* of God, then either there are no Christians but the *perfectly* holy, or the economy of grace has signally failed to accomplish an important object for which it was specifically intended! And if, through *actual* unbelief and hardness of heart in Christians, the economy of grace has thus failed so long to secure sinless perfection, according to its *design*, then how can it be proved, from the mere existence and conditional sufficiency of such an economy of grace, that any *do* attain to entire sanctification? To say that Christians *ought* to cease from sin from the first moment of their conversion, is nothing to the purpose. They undoubtedly *ought* from the first moment of moral action, from the beginning of accountable existence, however early it may be, to obey perfectly the Law of God, instead of *actually* having their "heart" so long "*fully set in them to do evil.*

2. *What is said respecting the New Covenant, proves too much, or it proves nothing.*

One of Mr. Mahan's leading arguments for the attainableness [attainment?] of entire sanctification, is this: "Perfection in holiness is *promised* to the Christian in the New Covenant, *under which he is now placed.*"—"The first, or Old Covenant, is the *Moral Law*, by which we are required to 'love the Lord our God with all our powers, and our neighbor as ourselves.'"—"What the Old Covenant *requires* of Christians, the New *promises* to them. For example: 1st. The Old Covenant requires *perfect* holiness."—"On the other hand, the New Covenant promises to the believer *perfect* holiness."—"Again 2d. The Old Covenant, or Moral Law, requires not only *perfect*, but *perpetual* holiness."— "The New Covenant, on the other hand, promises not only *perfect*, but *perpetual* holiness."—"We have evidence just as conclusive, that *perfect* and *perpetual* holiness is *promised* to Christians, as we have that it is *required* of them." See Mahan's Book, pp. 29—35.

Mr. Finney, too, says: "The Old Covenant was *mere Law*, to which was added a typical representation of the gospel."— "The second, or New Covenant, *is the writing of this Law in the heart.*"—"The Old Covenant required perfect obedience, on pain of death."—"The New Covenant is the *Causing* God's people to render perfect obedience." The word "*Causing,*" in this sentence, is *capitalized by* Mr. F. himself. Also, he says "The Old Covenant *required* a holy heart."—"The New is *the giving of* this holy heart."—"Obedience was enforced, under the Old Covenant, by penal sanctions."—"The New is the *production of* this obedience, by the Spirit of God."—"The Old Covenant promised life only upon the condition of perfect and perpetual obedience."—"The New is the *producing* of this perfect and perpetual obedience."—"The Old Covenant left men to the exercise of their *own strength*. The New is the *effectual* sanctification by the Holy Spirit."—"Here let me say, that this is one of the grand distinctions between the Old and New Covenants, that the New Covenant is the *effectual indwelling* of the Holy Spirit, *producing the very temper required by the Law, or Old Covenant.*"

Now if this proves anything to the purpose, does it not prove that every Christian, *as such,* has "*perfect* and *perpetual* holiness" given him—has "the Law written in his heart"—is "*Caused to render perfect obedience*"—has the "holy heart ('required by the Law') given him"—and has "the *effectual* indwelling of the Holy Spirit, producing *the very temper required by the Law, or Old Covenant?*" If the Old Covenant, or Moral Law, "left men to the exercise of their own strength," and the New is distinguished from it by "*causing God's people to render perfect obedience,*" by "being the *effectual* sanctification by the Holy Spirit," and "the producing of perfect and perpetual obedience;" and if (as Mr. Mahan says) the Christian is under this Covenant, we see not how there can be any, much less thousands of real saints, who are not entirely sanctified. Is not every *real* Christian sinlessly perfect? And are not all who are not perfect deceiving themselves, in thinking that they are Christians? And "if any man sin," ought he not to "*give up his hope,*" instead of saying, "we have an Advocate with the Father?" But if this New Covenant, as it is called, is conditioned on *previous* perfection in holiness—if the giving of a holy heart is conditioned on the exercise of *perfect* faith, working by *perfect* love, and *perfectly* purifying *the heart*—if "the causing God's people to render perfect obedience," is conditioned on the previous "surrender of their whole being to Christ," the "yielding up of *all their voluntary powers to the control of truth,*" or (O. Evan. vol. 1, p. 138) "the yielding up of their voluntary powers to the guidance, instruction, influences and government of the Holy Spirit," "their *whole being* to his influences and *control*"—if "the *effectual* indwelling," and "the *effectual* sanctification," are conditioned on all this being previously and *perfectly* done—what, we would ask, does the argument prove? Only that people would be perfect *if they were* perfect. If grace is so conditioned in the New Covenant, are not men left still "to the exercise of their *own strength,*" to their own unbelief and voluntary ignorance, in relation to an exceedingly important point touching the question of *actual* perfection in holiness—in relation to a *condition*, including the very blessing to be obtained? If it be said that this furnishes no valid excuse for continuance in sin; that men *ought* to be perfectly holy, we answer: It is even so. But what does this prove respecting *actual* entire sanctification? Not that it *is*, but *ought* to be attained. Indeed, neither "the New Covenant," nor the "provisions of the gospel," were *necessary* to take away all valid excuse for sin; or to make it the *duty* of all transgressors everywhere to repent and cease from sin forever. In the language of Dr. Griffin, "They still were complete moral agents, with full ability to perform their *whole* duty, *if rightly disposed.*" (Park Street Lectures, p. 23.) Yet, but for the Divine arrangement described in Rom. 8: 28—30, or in 2 Thes. 1: 13, or in Tit. 3: 5, no sinner would ever in fact repent. Ps. 14: 1—3; Eccl. 8: 11; John 6: 40.

3. *What they say of the responsibility of Christ, in relation to those who have received the New Covenant, or are entirely sanctified, proves too much for them, if it proves anything.*

From their own showing, there is no falling from a state of entire sanctification. A person entirely sanctified has of course received, with perfect faith, the New Covenant. Now Mr. Finney, (O. Evan. vol. 1, p. 105,) after a long course of reasoning to prove the point, says: "The New Covenant shall not be broken *by those who receive it.*" We have already seen that both Mr. F. and Mr. Mahan contend that "the New Covenant promises not only perfect, but *perpetual* holiness," or that it is "the producing of perfect and *perpetual* obedience." Not only so, Mr. M. (on p. 110) says: "When this is done; when there is that full and implicit reliance upon Christ, for the entire fulfilment of all that he has promised, he becomes directly *responsible* for our *full* and *complete* redemption."—"To us his word stands pledged to put the *laws* of God in our minds, and write them in our hearts"—"to give us one heart and one way, that we may fear God *forever*"—"to make an everlasting covenant with us that he will not turn *away from us*, to do us good, but that he will put the fear of God in our hearts, that we may not *depart from him*—finally, to sanctify us wholly, and preserve our whole spirit, and soul, and body, blameless unto the coming of our Lord Jesus Christ."

Mr. M. himself has explained abundantly, in his book, what *he* understands by the phraseology in this paragraph. It is impossible that he meant anything less than that "Christ becomes *directly responsible*," with "his word *pledged*," to keep those who receive, by *perfect faith*, the New Covenant, in a state of entire sanctification *forever*. But if Christ be thus responsible, in such a Covenant, can it be that any ever did or ever will fall from such a state?—It is not only absurd, but uncandid, to argue that because Adam fell from a sinless state, therefore persons entirely sanctified, to whom Christ's word is pledged to *keep them in that state,* may be believed to fall into sin. Why this reference so frequently to the case of Adam? Seeing that Adam, previous to his fall, had never been under the reigning power of sin, could he be said, *then,* to have been either partially or wholly *sanctified* in the sense in which this term is applied to Christ's people, to those who are *saved from their sins?* Had he then received the New Covenant? Had Christ become directly "responsible," with his "word pledged," to put "the laws of God in his mind and write them in his heart"—in short, to keep him in a state of sinless perfection? If not, then the case of Adam is not analogous. The same is true of the apostasy of the fallen angels. There was no covenant, no, word *pledged,* no *responsibility* binding God *to prevent it.* The question is not whether the entirely sanctified *might* sin again, *if* they were *inclined* to do so, but whether they *will* be inclined to sin—*disposed* to rebel against God—when, in solemn covenant the "word of Christ is pledged to put the Laws of God in their minds, and write them in their hearts;" to grant them "perfect and perpetual holiness;" in a word, to *prevent* their being *inclined* to sin, or *disposed* to rebel. How shocking, then, to hear it said of persons once in a state in which "the word of Christ was pledged to them," to "produce in them *perfect* and *perpetual obedience*"—to hear it said of *them,* that they, have nevertheless fallen into sin again! If there are any such persons, and they do thus fall, what pledge or surety have we that the glorified saints in Heaven will not defile their white robes, and be transformed into fiends? *If* Christ's word does indeed fail here, may it not fail *there* also? Says the Son of God (Luke 21: 33): "Heaven and earth shall pass away, but my word shall not pass away." Mr. Finney and Mr. Mahan are bound, therefore, in all logical propriety and consistency, either to give up their construction of the New Covenant, and their argument from it in favor of the doctrine of perfection in holiness *actually* attained; or to march boldly up, and take the positions which their premises include, viz. that all *real* Christians are entirely sanctified, and that, as such, they are to be kept in a state of "perfect and perpetual obedience" forever, by "*an indwelling Christ,*" who is "the perpetual Author of *all* their holy feelings and actions," and "the eternal life," or "holiness of the soul," and "*responsible*" to *prevent* their breaking the New Covenant. All this, unquestionably, their reasoning proves, if it proves anything to their purpose; and if they persist in its use, they are bound to follow it out, at least to its *direct* and *legitimate* conclusions. But if *they* do not, doubtless many of their *readers* will, though it shall lead them within less than "a Sabbath-day's journey" of one of the most abhorred positions of the "Antinomian Perfectionists."

4. *The argument from the petition in our Lord's prayer: "Thy will be done on earth as it is in Heaven," proves too much for their purpose, if it proves anything.*

Suppose that the term "will," here, denotes *preceptive* will—that the phrase, "be done on earth as it is in Heaven," means, "be done, by the dwellers on earth, as fully and as perfectly (according to their knowledge and capacity) as it is done by the inhabitants of Heaven;" and that the petition so understood, is *immediately* answered, as soon as it is offered in *perfect* faith, Now the will of God is perfectly done, not by a select few only, but by *all* the hosts of Heaven. If, therefore, we may emphasize the phrase, "*as it is in Heaven*," according to the necessity of the argument, we may also make it a prayer for the instantaneous entire sanctification of the whole world. Either, then, the whole world are entirely sanctified, or there are none that offer up this petition in perfect faith. But suppose the meaning to be narrowed so as to relate only to the Church of Christ on earth. Then *all Christians* at least, are entirely sanctified, if there is any one who prays, "Thy will be done," etc. in *perfect* faith, As soon as the disciples began to say, "Thy will be done on earth *as it is* in Heaven," Peter, and all the rest of them, were *at once* entirely sanctified, even though they were yet under the *Old Dispensation, if,* by any one, the prayer was made in perfect faith. At least, immediately on the introduction of the New Dispensation we may suppose *all* were entirely sanctified, so that at once *all* the true worshippers of God on earth began to do his "will" as perfectly, and as unanimously "*as it is*" done by his worshippers in Heaven. But were all true Christians in fact at once entirely sanctified, as soon as they were regenerated, even in the apostles' time? Were even Paul and Barnabus (Acts 15: 37—39) *both* entirely sanctified? Or those babes *in* Christ at Corinth? If not: why? Did none of the apostles or the disciples pray in *perfect faith?* What! not even *Paul,* nor *John,* nor those "perfect" ones at Philippi, so strenuously claimed as having been entirely sanctified? If there has been, in some respects, delay, or rather *progress,* in answering the petition, "Thy kingdom come;" if, as all must acknowledge, there has been *progress,* in many respects, in answering the petition, "Thy will be done on earth as it is in Heaven;" and especially, if the Great Head of the Church saw fit to direct us to pray daily, while *life lasts,* as suiting the real demands of our *actual* moral condition, "*Forgive us our sins, for we also forgive every one that is indebted to us,*" (Lu. 11: 4,) why attempt to infer from the Lord's prayer, that any, as soon as they are regenerated, or long before the close of probation, do in fact "*provisions;*" but upon *our exercising perfect faith.* But faith, as has already been remarked, works by *love, purifies the heart,* and *overcomes the world.* Acts 15: 9; Gal. 5: 6; 1 John 5: 4. *Perfect* faith therefore works by *perfect* love—*perfectly* purifies the heart—*perfectly* overcomes the world. *Perfect* faith implies the *perfection* of the other Christian graces. According to their own view of what is included in faith, it implies *present perfection in holiness.* How palpably absurd then to say! "Behold the sufficiency of the provisions of the gospel for our present entire sanctification! They are *such* that one has *only to go to Christ with perfect faith,* i. e. *only to go already perfect,* and then entire sanctification, or perfection in holiness, is at once the *result!*" So that sanctification, on this plan, turns out to be sanctification resulting from previous perfection in holiness—and the entirely sanctified make themselves *to differ* from others by their own exercise of *perfect* faith. And those who "testify" to their own entire sanctification, *may* testify quite as much to the *praise* of their own *perfect* faith, as to the glory of the grace of Christ. One *might* say: "On such a day I went with perfect faith—with all my voluntary powers yielded up to the control of truth'—with my *whole being* surrendered to Christ'—with my *heart purified,* and the *world under my feet*—to the Son of God; and then, through the riches of his grace, I *became* (in proportion to my knowledge and capacity) just as holy as *I was before!*" Alas, how little additional glory is the Saviour likely to receive by this theory, as "a *perfect* Redeemer," and as "the Author of a *full* salvation," etc.! Indeed, if the gospel provisions are only, in *such a sense,* sufficient for our entire sanctification in "the progress of this life," and are *thus* conditioned, is it not absolutely amazing that any—much more that men of *logical* minds—should attempt to draw thence an argument—their favorite and strongest argument—for the doctrine of *sinless perfection attained?*

But Mr. Finney argues, that if nothing can be proved from these *conditionally* sufficient provisions of the gospel, in regard to actual entire sanctification, then we cannot prove that any will be *actually* saved, seeing that salvation is conditioned on repentance and faith, or on obedience to the gospel. At this, too, we marvel. If God's "*effectual calling*" of sinners to repentance, to faith, to holiness, and *thus* to salvation, were *conditioned* on their *previously* repenting—believing—obeying, then the argument would have some force. But it was God's promise in the Covenant of Redemption, his purpose from eternity—not with an *if—effectually* to call, to justify, and finally to glorify those who were ordained to eternal life; and as soon shall his throne pass away, as one jot or one tittle of his revealed promise or purpose fail of fulfilment. See e. g. Is. 53: 10—12; 2 Tim. 1: 9; Acts 13: 48; Rom. 8: 29—30. Let Mr. F. prove attain to sinless perfection? And why attempt to convince us that those who "are morally just as perfect as God," need to say, from day to day, "*Forgive* us our sins, which were long since confessed, forsaken and *forgiven?*" As well might Abraham, and other saints in Paradise, continue to say, "*Forgive us our sins.*" No doubt the glorified saints in Heaven will forever detest their former transgressions, while they gratefully sing:— "Unto Him that loved us, and washed us from our sins in his own blood, and hath made us kings and priests unto God and his Father; to him be glory and dominion forever and ever." But how incongruous to continue the prayer: "*Forgive* us our sins" long since *remitted* and *washed away* through the blood of the Lamb!

Should it be argued, as we have heard it, that a person must be at least "very spiritual," to be able to subjoin, "*for we also forgive every one that is indebted to us;*" we reply. 1st. That individuals, without even being Christians at all, have been known to declare, with probable sincerity, that they were not *conscious* of exercising any feeling of malice, or of revenge, toward any human being. 2d. That, if the expression referred to implies *perfection* in holiness, then none but the *perfect* can innocently offer the petition; and they, by implication, say: "Forgive us our *sins*, for now we are *sinless*." 3d. That those who can see no difference, even in degree, between freedom from feelings of revenge, or spite, or ill-will, and *positively* loving God with *all* our powers, and our neighbor as ourselves, construe and appreciate the broad claims of Jehovah's Law differently from what we do. All young converts to God might say: "We forgive every one that is indebted to us." Has it come to this, then, that the standard of entire sanctification is brought down to where babes in Christ *begin* to "grow in grace?" Touching the petition: "Thy will be done on earth," etc. we have seen, that, in many respects, it is answered only progressively. May it not, then, in relation to *personal* holiness (supposing the petition to relate to this) be progressively, and at last *perfectly* answered, in respect to every one of God's people, by *completing* in each of them the work of sanctification while on earth, though it be at the *instant*, of departing to be with other "spirits of just men made perfect?" Be this as it may, we are confident that no argument favorable to the doctrine of sinless perfection attained *amid* the saint's probation, can be extorted from it, that shall not prove too much, if it proves anything.

5. *The same is true of the argument from* 1 *Thes* 5: 23, "*And the very God of peace sanctify you wholly; and I pray God your whole spirit and soul and body be preserved blameless unto the coming of our Lord Jesus Christ.*" Compare Lu. 1: 6; 1 Thes. 4: 3—7.

We need not stop to remark, that the words, "*I pray God,*"

are supplied by the translator; or to inquire whether the phrase, "sanctify you wholly"—*hagiasai humas holoteleis*—was intended to imply absolute perfection in holiness; or "blameless," to signify *sinless*; or "*unto* the coming," etc.—*en te parousia*—to convey no meaning but the one which Mr. Finney and Mr. Mahan derive from it. We will suppose that the apostle intended it as a prayer for the present entire sanctification of "the church of the Thessalonians," to whom he was writing. The apostle adds: "Faithful is he that calleth you, who also will do it;" i. e. (according to the supposition) "will now, at once, entirely sanctify you—all of you, to whom I am writing," But do Mr. Finney and Mr. Mahan believe that all the members of the Thessalonian church were at once entirely sanctified, on the utterance, by Paul, of that "prayer?" The prayer was not for one, or two, or a few only, but for the church—all the members of the church, "The God of peace sanctify you wholly." The apostle was accustomed to pray much for all the churches, See e. g. Rom. 1: 9; Eph. 3: 14—21; Col. 1: 9—14; Heb. 13: 20. If he held the Oberlin theory of instantaneous sanctification, it is not likely that he failed to pray that the Romans, the Ephesians, and other Christians, as well as the Thessalonians, might be at once entirely sanctified—adding, "Faithful is he that calleth you, who also will do it." But was it so done?— Were they all thus sanctified? If "the Faithful" did not so "do it" for all, is there any evidence that he so "did it" for any? If the prayer for their entire sanctification at once, failed of fulfilment in respect to some, may it not have failed in respect to all? There is not a particle of evidence that one of the Thessalonians was immediately sanctified entirely, in answer to that prayer. While there is conclusive evidence (2 Thes. 3: 11) that at least some of them were not. Were the Ephesians immediately brought to perfection in holiness, in answer to Paul's prayer for them? See Rev. 2: 4. Are Messrs. Finney and Mahan certain, then, after all, that Paul expected the present, instantaneous entire sanctification of the Thessalonians? If he did, why were they not all immediately made perfect in holiness? Did not Paul pray "according to the will of God?" Mr. F. and Mr. M. delight to repeat the expression: "This is the *will* of God, even *your* sanctification," addressed to these very Thessalonians.— Or did not Paul pray in faith—perfect faith? Mr. Finney says Paul "was an extravagant boaster," for saying certain things, some of which were directed to this very church, "if he was not sinless." Did not he (if "entirely sanctified") pray in perfect faith, knowing that "this was the will of God, even *their*" immediate entire "sanctification?" Or does this argument, so often repeated, dwindle away at last to this: That the Thessalonians and others *ought* to have lived without sin; and that *if* they had gone to Christ with perfect faith, with "all their voluntary powers yielded up to the control of truth," etc. they would have been entirely sanctified? Then, as we have repeatedly seen, it proves nothing to the purpose for which it is adduced.

6. The same is true, too, of the argument from the declaration (Eph. 3: 20,) that God is *"able to do exceeding abundantly above all that we ask or think."*

Mr. Mahan asks: "When we pray for this," i. e. immediate entire sanctification in this life, "or any other blessing, do not the scriptures authorize us to expect more than we *"ask or think?"*—"But Mr. Folsom's theory would require us to expect less than we ask and think." See Am. Bib. Repos. for October, 1840, p. 416. The apostle had just described his prayer for the Ephesian church, (3: 14—19.)—Mr. M. says that Paul prayed for "this specific blessing," viz. *present* entire sanctification. But if the apostle prayed for this blessing, it must have been intended for the Ephesians. For them, and not for himself, was he praying. He asked, then, for the immediate, entire sanctification of those to whom his epistle was directed—the church of Ephesus; and he "expected" more than he "asked or *thought."* If so, did the results, the immediate results, correspond with his expectation? Were all the Ephesian Christians made, at once, "morally just as perfect as God?" And was anything "more than" the blessing of entire sanctification for which "he asked," immediately granted? If so, what favor did the Ephesians receive, that was not "asked," nor "thought of," by Paul, who "was an 'extravagant boaster," if he did not himself enjoy at that time, the blessings of entire sanctification? Was it a renovation of their "debilitated powers"—a "complete restoration of their bodies to primitive physical perfection," like that "before the fall?" For this, though *"dreamed of"* since his day, we have no reason to believe was "thought of" by Paul, and *might* therefore have been a blessing not "asked" for them, by the apostle. Or were some, besides *all* the Ephesian church, "caused" at once "to render perfect obedience"—some that Paul, though "sinless," and so fully enlightened in respect to the economy of grace, did not think of, as those who would receive that blessing? But Mr. Mahan asks: "Do not the scriptures authorize us to expect more than we ask or think," "when we pray for this or any other blessing?" This species of logic is not original with Mr. M. It has long been in use among the Universalists to prove the doctrine that all men will finally be made holy and happy. They have been able to make it, in their cause, quite as strong an *argumentum ad captandum* as Mr. M. has in his. Mr. Mahan argues, that Paul prayed for the entire and permanent sanctification of *some* in this life—that "this is the will of God, even" the present complete "sanctification" of *some*—that God is *"able to do more than we ask or think;"* and that, therefore, *some* are made perfectly and permanently holy in this world. The Universalist argues, that Paul (1 Tim. 2: 1—4) directs that "first of all, supplications, prayers, intercessions and giving of thanks be made for *all men*"—that "this is good and acceptable in the sight of God our Saviour, who will have *all men* to be saved and to come to the knowledge of the truth"—that "God is able to do more than we ask or think"—and that therefore all men will be made holy and happy. In respect to the application of the passage under consideration, the Universalist has the advantage not only of originality, but of *plausibility*, over Mr. Mahan. He might say: "*We* ask and look for the holiness and happiness of *all men*, but *your* "theory would require us to expect less than we ask and think." It is true, indeed, that this proves too much even for the Universalist. For it is conceivable, and in one sense exceedingly desirable, that all men should be made heirs of Heaven, by being made perfectly holy and perfectly happy during their entire existence, instead of having any moral defilement, or any pain, or trouble in this world. So that any one, crazy enough to advocate the doctrine of *no sin nor misery*, in this world, nor in the world to come, *because* "God is love," and is "able to do more than we ask or think," might say to the Universalist, "I have the advantage of you: for your theory requires us to expect *less* than we ask and think." But the logic of the Universalist is as conclusive as Mr. Mahan's. It overlooks, as Mr. M's does, man's free agency, and his abuse of that free agency. The Universalist may indeed show that "provision" is made *conditionally* for the salvation of all men—that God "commands all men every where to repent"—that he would have all men to be saved, by complying with the *conditions* of salvation; but all *this*, so far from proving *actual* universal salvation, does not prove that any will in fact be saved—that any will obey the gospel. We do indeed believe that a great multitude, which no man can number, out of all nations and kindreds and people and tongues, will stand before the throne and cry: "Salvation to our God and to the Lamb." But our belief that they will thus stand, "with white robes and palms in their hands," is founded (as we have shown) upon evidence, clear, direct and conclusive, that it is, and therefore has *always* been the purpose of the Omniscient and Unchangeable, effectually to incline some of the human family to comply (of course, freely) with the *terms* of salvation; and that he does in fact "save *some*" (2 Tim. 1: 9), calling them with an holy calling, not according to their works; but according to his own purpose and grace, which was given them in Christ Jesus before the world began." Can Mr. Mahan show, in the same way, that it is God's purpose *effectually* to incline some to avail themselves (with perfect faith, etc.) of the provisions of the gospel, made conditionally sufficient for their present entire sanctification, and actually to "cause of probation, in which—after receiving "*spiritual eyes*"—God's people are not *at once* so sanctified, and raised above the reach of every temptation, as to be wholly *prevented* from falling into any degree of sin—of a state in which they are led to see with horror the plague of their hearts—the power, the insidiousness, and the multitudinous workings of their terrible moral malady; and thus to realize more fully the extent of redemption which they need, and which they are in the process of receiving from day to day, while "looking unto Jesus, the author and finisher of their faith;" and exercising themselves in conflict with the world, the flesh and the devil—humbled under the chastenings of the Lord, and strengthened and disciplined amid the varied trials which they meet. For many reasons, it is important that the saint *realize* the depravity of his own heart, and the immense debt of gratitude which he owes to the Saviour. In Luke 7: 41—47, our Lord strikingly illustrates the principle, that love to him is in proportion to the *sense* of sin forgiven. The High and Lofty One who inhabiteth eternity—and "with whom one day *is* as a thousand years, and a thousand years as one day"—*may*, therefore, have wise reasons for *so* saving his people from their sins as to cause them deeply to feel their intense *need* of such salvation, and to utter—each of them—with an humble and penitent heart, the sentiment:

> "Oh to grace how *great* a debtor,
> *Daily* I'm constrained to be;"

and in the world of glory to have their joy and gratitude increased by their full *realization* of the tremendous corruption of heart from which they have been saved.

Payson, speaking of his spiritual trials, says: "I find that the depths of Satan, and of a heart desperately wicked, are not so easily fathomed. These unfathomable depths, however, only serve to show me more clearly *the infinite heights and depths of Christ's love.*"—This accords with the experience of other eminent saints. That God *may*—in order to *show men their hearts* and *humble* them—leave them to sin, i. e. not *prevent* their sinning, is made indubitably certain in his word. For example, we are told expressly that "God left Hezekiah to try him, that he *might know all that was in his heart,*" and that he permitted (i. e. did not *prevent*) the wandering of the children of Israel in the wilderness forty years—"to *humble* them and to *prove* them and to *know what was in their heart,* whether they would keep his commandments or no."—It is not asserted that the people of God are m re humble *while* sinning, or that it is proper for them to "do evil that good may come," although God does cause "*the wrath of man to praise him,*" and "*restrain the remainder*" thereof. *While* Hezekiah was displaying before the ambassadors of the king of Babylon, "all the house of his precious

things," and "all the house of his armor, and all that was found
in his treasures," his heart was lifted up with pride—but when
led to discern his sinfulness, he humbled himself exceedingly
low "under the mighty hand of God."—Peter, too, while "curs-
ing and swearing" and denying Christ, was far from being humble; but afterwards, when his Lord had "turned and looked
upon him," and he was brought to *realize* his vileness, "he went
out and wept bitterly." His sad and shameful denial was made,
by the grace of God, the *occasion* of destroying his high self-
confidence—of deeply and mercifully humbling him.

It is worthy of remark, that on the Oberlin theory, probation
virtually closes with the reception of the New Covenant, or as
soon as entire sanctification is attained. That is, an entirely
sanctified person "*knows*," by "*the highest kind of evidence*,"
that he *is* thus sanctified; and he is as *certain*, therefore, as he
can be of anything, that "a *confirmed* state of pure and perfect holiness, such as the first covenant, or Moral Law demands,"
"the pardon of all sin, or perfect justification," and "the perpetual fruition of the Divine presence and favor," are *pledged*
to him in solemn covenant, never, by *either* of the parties, to
be broken. All this he is supposed to *know*. He may now look
upon his soul, as "the spirit of a just one made perfect." He
lingers on earth as a *resident graduate* of the school of probation, having, as his diploma, the "New Covenant," which
"promises" to those who receive it, "*perfect and perpetual holiness*." And if he continues to use "the means of grace,"
adapted to a state of *trial*, it must be the "result of a happy
inconsistency with his principles." To his *own mind* there can
be no more *doubt* or *contingency*, touching his perseverance in
perfect holiness, and his "perpetual fruition of the Divine presence and favor," than to a saint in glory, respecting *his* future
perseverance and bliss. He cannot, therefore, be said to be in a
state of probation, in any sense not just as applicable to the present condition of Abraham or Paul. His *present* character is,
by the theory, supposed to be *certainly known* to *himself* as well
as to God, and what his character *will be* forever—indubitably
ascertained. The proper idea of probation, then, is excluded.
We might here inquire, whether one who fully adopts this theory
and *thinks* himself to be in a state of entire sanctification, can
be expected to "work out his own salvation with fear and trem-
bling"—to "give diligence *to make* his calling and election
sure"—to be watchful, prayerful, humble, and disposed to self-
examination?—and whether neglect of appointed means of
grace—spiritual pride—censoriousness—and contempt of wholesome rules and established order, are not natural results of such
a delusion?* We might ask, also: Is one likely to hunger and

* It is not a little impertinent to reply to this, by asking: "Can entire

thirst after righteousness, who believes that he is already filled?
He might reasonably seek to enlarge his *capacity*, but not to fill
that which he thinks is full.—Will one who fancies that he is
"as free from all sin as the Lord Jesus Christ," be apt to realize
his need of "purifying himself even as he is pure?"—of cleansing that which he supposes to be no longer unclean?—And will
one who imagines that the last of the Canaanites is dead or driven
out, and that "there remaineth no more land to be possessed,"
be inclined still to gird himself to the war, and "slay the slain,"
and take what he dreams that he has already in full possession?"

8. *Another fallacious argument—consisting in a wrong meaning given to a word, and in a false analogy; and proving too
much, if it proves anything.*

Mr. Mahan says, on p. 54 of his Book: "Every Christian,
also, admits that no one can be saved, who does not aim at perfection. Now to aim at this state, with the belief that it is unat-
tainable, is an absolute impossibility. To *aim* at the accom-
plishment of an object, is the same thing as to *intend* to accomplish it. How can a man intend to do that which he regards as
impracticable? Let the hunter, for example, if he can, point
his weapon at the moon, with the intention of hitting it. He
will find the formation of such intention, with his present belief
of the power of his weapon, and the distance of the object, an
impossibility."

Were the occasion fitting, we might here say, that, considering the extraordinary progress of mind in this age, when so
many systems of philosophy are vanishing away, it would be
nothing remarkable if some hunter—or at least some enterpriz-
ing theologue—thinking that "heretofore" the moon had "been
set *too high*," or *too far off*, and that it is in fact only a few
rods distant—should point his weapon at her silvery face, with
the intention of hitting it. A great poet represents a certain
personage as saying:

——"Methinks it were an *easy leap*,
To pluck bright honor from the pale-faced moon;"

but whether this was owing to the individual's entertaining peculiar views respecting the height of the moon, or to the belief
that less vigor would be required of him, in such a leap, on account of his powers being "debilitated by transgression;" or
whether he supposed that *if* he should *"only"* first leap to the
moon, he would *then be there* just as long as he *actually remained
there*—we are not particularly informed. We proceed, however,
to state some graver objections to Mr. Mahan's argument.

sanctification, or perfection in holiness, make its possessor proud, censori-
ous," etc.?—No intelligent person ever said that it did.

Entire sanctification is one thing—the delusion, that one *is* entirely sanctified, when he *is not*, is altogether another thing.

(1.) He defines the word *aim* to mean *intend*, i. e. as implying purpose with *expectation*. Hence, to say that a person *aims*, i. e. purposes and *expects* to do what he does *not expect* to do, is a contradiction in terms.

But when the Christian is said to aim at perfection, it is meant that he *endeavors*, or *strives after* it. It is no contradiction to say, that one *endeavors* to come up to a standard without *expecting* fully to attain to it. Many a child, for example, while learning to write, *endeavors* to imitate letter after letter of the elegant copy before him without *expecting* then or ever to equal it.—Dr. Franklin relates of himself that at a certain time, when desirous of improving in composition, he obtained and read a volume of the Spectator; and being enchanted with its style, " wished it were in *his power to imitate* it."—" With this view," says he, " I selected some of the papers, made short summaries of the sense of each period, and put them for a few days aside. I then, without looking at the book, *endeavored* to restore the essays to their due form, and to express each thought at length as it was in the original, employing the most appropriate words that occurred to my mind." This species of endeavor he continued some time, and found it to be a means of considerable improvement. "This," says he, "encouraged me to hope that I should succeed in time in writing decently in the English language." From this it is evident,

(1.) That Franklin *aimed* or "endeavored" each time to equal the style of the Spectator. That was his aim and that his standard. To that were his powers directed from week to week.

(2.) That he did not *expect*, each hour, to come up, *then*, fully to that standard. Even after considerable practice, and no small success, he was only " encouraged to hope"—i. e. in some degree, to expect—"that he should succeed in time"—not immediately—"in writing *decently in the English language.*" We know of some others who could testify, from "consciousness," that they have *aimed* or *endeavored*, day after day, during certain periods of their lives, to come up to a certain standard of literary excellence, without *expecting* then, or ever, to fall in no respect short of it. Every scholar will, in this connection, be reminded of the great Roman orator's *aliquid immensum infinitumque*. or lofty *beau ideal* of excellence, which was so habitually and vividly before his " mind's eye," that though he often thrilled and astonished others, himself he could never satisfy, even by his happiest efforts.

But to return to Mr. M's illustration of the hunter. We have heard of hunters possessing such skill, in the use of the rifle, as to be able, in the evening, to snuff a candle several rods distant four times out of seven. They *sometimes* hit the mark; but this is not *absolute perfection*. That consists in *never failing to hit the mark*. Now supposing that no man ever did, or ever

will, attain to such perfect skill, in the use of. the rifle, as to hit
such a mark *every* time—would there be any absurdity in saying that a person endeavors or aims to hit the mark every time,
without expecting *never* to fail of hitting it?—Perfection in holiness consists in hitting, unfailingly and exactly, all the number-
less points which come within the wide scope of God's broad and
spiritual Law. On the Oberlin principle referred to already, a
man would be only in a state of partial sanctification, though he
should *frequently* will right, i. e. hit the mark. To be entirely
sanctified, implies that one *never fails* to hit the mark.

(3.) Mr. M's illustration of the hunter pointing his weapon at
the moon, has the appearance of being selected for mere *effect*.
This may not, however, have been intended. The illustration
is one of the numerous examples of *false analogy*, which abound
in his book. A palpable natural impossibility is employed as
analogous to the certainty of moral imperfection in man, arising
from the *lack of right disposition*. Now did Mr. M. intend to
convey the idea, that according to the views commonly received,
it is in the same sense impossible for a man perfectly to obey
God, that it is, in the case supposed, to hit the moon?—The
manner in which he uses the terms "impracticable" and "unat-
tainable," in the same connection with the illustration, would
indicate that such was his intention. Has he, then, forgot the
distinction—assumed in the Bible, and recognized by Edwards,
Dwight, Griffin and others—between *natural* and *moral* inability?—between a natural *impossibility*, excluding both the reality
and the sense of moral obligation—and an *indisposition*, or defect of inclination, resulting in the certainty of not coming up
perfectly to the requirements of a Law which the conscience
assents to as right?—Surely the inability of Joseph's brethren,
to "speak peaceably unto him," (Gen. 37: 4,) or of the children
of Israel to "serve the Lord," (Josh. 24: 19,) or of the Christian to "hit" exactly every point embraced within the comprehensive demands of the Moral Law, (Rom. 7: 18—23; Gal. 5:
17,) is not to be confounded with the inability of Mr. M's hunter
to hit the moon. Mr. M., we presume, does not ordinarily overlook this very important distinction. Yet his language is, in
this instance, fitted to mislead the unwary reader. And the
more so, as he at least intimates, in the same connection, that
not to *expect* or *believe* that we shall do a thing, is equivalent to
an *impossibility* of doing that thing—i. e. that to "think it absolutely *certain* that we never will perform" a thing, is synony-
mous with "regarding it as *impracticable*."

We would here say, that whatever may be the meaning of Mr.
M.—the only question which our views require us to discuss,
touching the subject of *expectation*, is this: Does our not *expecting* to live, in this world, "as free from all sin as did our Lord
Jesus Christ," affect our relation to the government of God—to

duty—and to conscience—in the same way as would a *natural impossibility?*—In order to understand the question, let us inquire what is properly meant by *expectation.* "Expectation," says Dr. Webster, "is the act of expecting or looking forward to a future event, with at least some *reason to believe that the event will happen.* Expectation differs from hope. Hope originates in desire, and may exist with little or no ground of belief that the desired event will arrive. Expectation is founded on some *reasons which render the event probable.*" Let it be borne in mind, then, that expectation, properly so called, is neither a vague wish or hope merely; nor the *cause* of the event looked for, but an *effect*—a conviction, or belief, produced by evidence, by facts showing the probability of the thing expected. In the order of cause and effect, it is not expectation of sinning; that gives man his propensity to wander from God, but the evidence of this dreadful propensity, with its tremendous results reaching round the globe and from generation to generation, which produces the expectation of its continuing to be a mournful truth, in all ages, that "there is not a just man upon earth that doeth good and *sinneth not*"—that "in many things we all offend." All men everywhere are under obligation infinitely strong to live in all respects to the glory of God. But whether we ought to *expect* that any will, in fact, so live, depends upon there being, or not being, *ground* to *believe* that the event will actually happen. Expectation, if just and reasonable, is according to evidence. Hence, although all sin is forbidden and wrong, yet it is no virtue, but delusion, to expect that all, or that any will in fact be so pure, in the course of the present life, as to say truly, "we have no sin," if there is no *reason* to believe that any will be thus pure. Therefore, if it is not true that any will in fact live as free from all sin, in the progress of this life, as did our Saviour, there is no merit, but manifest folly, in believing that they will. We will now suppose that a Christian is considering whether he ought, or ought not to *expect* that he shall in fact, in this world, exercise stronger faith than Abraham, more enduring patience than Job, more exemplary meekness than Moses, more scrupulous adherence to principle than Daniel—"in a word, be in his measure as perfect as God is." The question is not whether he *ought to be* sinlessly perfect; but whether he *ought to expect* that he shall actually be so. Now if it be true, that he is going *to be* thus perfect, and he has *evidence* that he is, then he is bound to *expect* such an event. But if it be not true, or if there be no evidence that it is, he is not bound to expect it, unless it be supposed that he ought to believe what is not true, or what there is no reason to believe. We will suppose that the individual is looking for evidence bearing upon the question of fact before him. Is it true that he is going to live henceforth, while on earth, as free from all sin as did the

Lord Jesus Christ? He ought so to live, but that does not prove that he will. He sincerely resolves to endeavor to do his whole duty. But this has long been the genuine and leading purpose of his heart, and yet he has " in many things offended."—He then looks into the Bible to see whether any of the saints therein described, did in fact so live. He does indeed find some few strong expressions applied to Paul and others, whom different classes of Perfectionists have claimed as sinless, but he finds still stronger expressions applied to Job—to David—to Zacharias—and some others, who are known to have been not in a state of entire sanctification. He perceives, too, that not only the general tenor of the word of God, but explicit declarations made by the individuals thus claimed, are evidently inconsistent with the supposition of their having attained to that state. Leaving the Bible, he looks into Mr. Mahan's Book on Christian Perfection, and into the Oberlin Evangelist. He reads about "the provisions of the gospel"—"full salvation"—"complete redemption"—and "the New Covenant;" and is taught that *if* he will *only* exercise *perfect faith*. etc. he shall be in a state of entire sanctification. But alas, that "*if*," and that very comprehensive "*only*."—Is it true that he will in fact perpetually exercise *perfect faith*—maintain the "surrender of his whole being to Christ," and continually " yield up all his voluntary powers to the *control of truth?*"—If it is, then he ought to expect it. But if it is not true, then to expect it, is to believe a falsehood; and is what can have no tendency to promote his growth in grace, unless it be admitted that God will sanctify through the belief of a falsehood. The truth that he will fall short of loving God continually, with all his heart—soul—mind, and strength, and his neighbor as himself, is one for which he feels responsible—over which he mourns daily—on account of which he often "abhors himself."—But still it *is* a truth—and the clear and multiplied evidence of this truth, produces the expectation, and not the expectation the truth—that he will, while on earth, be, in his measure, less perfect than God is.

The philosophical order—or the order of cause and effect—is this:—1st. The Cause. Man's awful proneness to sin—the abundant *evidence* of the truth, that while he continues to dwell in this world, he will fall, in some degree, short of entire sinlessness. 2d. The Effect. *Expectation*, or belief in accordance with that evidence. That is, *because it is true that men will be*, in some degree, imperfect, we *expect* that *they will be*. How manifest is it, then, that our not *expecting* that we shall obey God perfectly, does not affect our relation to his government—to duty—and to conscience, as would a *natural impossibility of obeying him*. To illustrate the principle by a strong case, suppose that a drunkard, after several unavailing resolutions to abstain, becomes convinced, that though present and eternal ruin awaits him, he shall not in fact reform. Now is it not still his duty to reform? Does his *expectation* force him against his will to drink? No. He is not sufficiently *inclined* to be a sober man. He *voluntarily* obeys the calls of appetite rather than the voice of God and his conscience. He *will* not break away from his thraldom. And it is the evidence which he has that such is, on the whole, his wicked *choice*, and will continue to be, that produces his *expectation* of not reforming. The evil then is not to be charged to the expectation, but to the facts which justify that expectation. But, to take another and stronger case of expecting to continue in sin. Mr. Mahan at least will not deny that Satan *is* a moral agent, under obligation to repent and become perfectly holy. Nor will he deny that that proud spirit, with a heart fully set in him to do evil, believes it to be perfectly certain that he shall be a sinner forever, under the wrath of God. Now is this, his expectation that he shall in fact continue to sin, equivalent to a *natural impossibility* of obeying his Creator? If so, is it his duty to become holy—i. e. to do what is naturally impossible? Mr. M. will not say that it is. But if it is not his duty to repent, he violates no *obligation* by continuing impenitent. But to violate no obligation is to be *sinless;* and then Satan would be *sinless* in his continued rebellion against his Creator. This neither Mr. M. nor any one else believes. We would moreover ask whether this expectation, that he will in fact continue to sin, affords the same relief to his violated conscience, as would even the *belief* that it was naturally *impossible* for him to obey God?

(4.) Besides, Mr. M's doctrine of expectation really brings down the rule of action to a level with one's present performances. That is, according to this doctrine, one cannot *aim* to do what he does not *expect* to do. Of course he cannot *aim* to do to-day what he does not *expect* to do to-day. Mr. M's hunter, for example, cannot *aim* to hit a mark to day, unless he *expects* to hit it to-day. He cannot aim to hit it to-day, merely because he expects to acquire such skill as to hit the mark by an aim which he may take next week. Now if this principle be true, the Christian aims each day at no higher standard than he expects to come up to that day. His expectation of what he shall in fact do at any given time, is then his standard. But as expectation of what we shall do each day, is founded upon *those things only which go to show what we shall be likely in fact to do,* our expectation, i. e. the standard of our *aim,* is naturally brought down to a level with our *actual performances during any given period.* If the Christian, then, must aim each day of his life at perfection—and if he can aim only at what he *expects* actually to do—then what he *expects to do,* and not the unchanging Law of God, is his standard of perfection. And he is perfect according to this principle, if he does all that he expects actually to do. In this connection we remark:

1. That where the doctrine of expecting that we shall in fact live in this world as free from all sin as our Saviour did, is speciously and zealously inculcated, some will be led to believe that they themselves so live. In the O. Evan. vol. 2, p. 49, Mr. Finney himself incidentally discloses the fact, that there are some at Oberlin considered as in a state of entire sanctification. Mr. Mahan has admitted the same fact.

2. That taking men as they are, and are likely to be, the natural tendency of this doctrine is to degrade the standard of perfection immeasurably below the elevation at which it was viewed by Isaiah, Paul and Edwards, who, notwithstanding their great attainments, considered themselves so far beneath it. We have already quoted a declaration of Mr. Finney, which shews how the adoption of this theory is affecting his own views of the Law of God. "I cannot but feel that much of the difficulty that good men have upon this subject," [of persons claiming that they render entire obedience to the Moral Law.] "has arisen out of a comparison of the lives of saints with a standard *entirely above* that which the Law of God does or can demand of persons in all respects in our circumstances." He also more than intimates. (on p. 26 of the O. Evan. vol. 2) that some who had really attained to a state of entire sanctification, did not recognize the fact, on account of their incorrect views of such a state. That is, we are left to infer that if Mrs. President Edwards—instead of being misled by that great and good man, her husband—could have had her mind so enlightened, by studying the views of Pelagius, or certain Lectures which have been delivered since her day, as to believe that "that which first leads us into sin is our innocent constitution, *just as* it was the innocent constitution of Adam to which the temptation was addressed that led him into sin," she would have seen that she was entirely sanctified. It is possible, too, that if the President himself—instead of viewing the Law of God in its elevation, where Job and Isaiah beheld it with such deep self-abasement—had seen it lowered down with a more accommodating nearness to the realities of human frailty, he would not have exclaimed, "I know not how to express better what my sins appear to me to be, than by heaping infinite upon infinite, and multiplying infinite by infinite;" but would have begun to testify to his own entire sanctification! We remark.

3. That it is an exceedingly great mistake to suppose that the tendency of the Oberlin theory is to introduce a higher standard of piety in the Church. It has often and perhaps honestly been asserted, that—touching the subject of sanctification—the grand difference between its friends and others, is their *setting the standard of Christian character higher than the rest of God's people.* Precisely the reverse of this is true. The standard of character is God's Law. A theory, then, which so very strongly tempts its advocates to lower down the claims of that broad and spirit-

ral Law, must of course tend to degrade, instead of elevating the standard of character. This theoretical tendency has, perhaps without a single exception in the history of the Church, been proved by corresponding practical results.

We are under no temptation to underrate Mr. Finney's former labors and distinguished success in revivals. The temptation, so far as the defence of our views is concerned, is all on the other side. Nothing would suit the ends of our argument better, than to set forth, in bold relief, his various excellencies as a revival preacher, and to draw a veil over whatever tended to mar his usefulness in the Church of Christ. The power with which he used to hold up the Law of God, and the energy and deep feeling with which he so often described the moral distance of the best saints on earth, from perfect conformity to that lofty standard, are remembered by some of us with admiration. During the entire period of his great success in revivals, when he laid the foundation of all his reputation and influence in the churches, he rejected with abhorrence the doctrine of *sinless perfection attained* in this life. This is known by those who then heard him. Not only so, the very last of his course of Lectures on Revivals, delivered at New York in the winter of 1834—5, contains evidence very full and decisive on this point. This Lecture is on "Growth in Grace," and has in it so many excellent things that we would commend it, at this juncture, to the prayerful and candid perusal of Christians seeking instruction on this subject. He declares that "to grow in grace is to *increase* in a spirit of conformity to the will of God, and to govern our conduct *more* and *more* by the same principles that God does."—"It is manifest," says he, "that where a professor gets the idea that he is growing *rapidly* in grace, it is a suspicious circumstance. For the best of reasons. To grow better, implies a more clear and distinct knowledge of the breadth of God's Law, and a growing sense of the sinfulness of sin. But the more clear an individual's views become of the standard, *the lower* will be the estimate which he forms of himself, because the clearer will be his views of the distance at which he still is from that pure and perfect standard of holiness to which God requires him to conform all his conduct. If he compares himself with a *low standard*, he will think he is doing pretty well."—"I have always observed this to be true, that when persons are making, in reality, the most rapid advances in holiness, they have the most debasing views of themselves, and the humblest sense of their state. I do not mean that those who understand the subject, and who know what are evidences of growth in grace, may not, by *reasoning* or by *comparing* their present with their former views, feelings, and character, come to the conclusion that they are growing in grace." [How different this from certainly knowing their state, by the *direct testimony of consciousness*, "the high-

any kind of evidence!] "But that if they should determine, simply by their *present views* of what they are, and what God requires, if they should not *reason* on the subject, they would come to the conclusion that they were growing worse and worse. Individuals who were making rapid progress, have often felt so, because they saw more and more clearly the standard with which they are to compare themselves."—Speaking of Job, he observes: "God had said he was a perfect and an upright man. He did not mean that Job was perfectly sinless; for it was not true that he was perfect in this sense. But God meant to say that he was *sincere*. This is the meaning of the word perfect here; and it is generally the meaning of it in the Bible. He meant to say that Job was honest in religion. Job remained in this darkness, and all the while justifying himself, for a long time; but by and by he had clear views of God, and all his self-justification was gone, and he cried out, 'I have heard of thee by the hearing of the ear, but now mine eye seeth thee; wherefore I abhor myself, and repent in dust and ashes.' Such deep self-abasement was the natural result of clear views of God. So it was with Isaiah. *I have been confounded when I have heard some persons talk of their purity, and of being entirely pure from their sins, and of being perfect.* They must have vastly different views of themselves from what Job and Isaiah had. What did Isaiah see? He says: 'I saw the Lord sitting upon a throne high and lifted up, and his train filled the temple. Above it stood the seraphim; each one had six wings; with twain he covered his face, and with twain he covered his feet, and with twain he did fly. And one cried unto another and said, Holy, *Holy*, HOLY is the Lord of hosts; the whole earth is full of his glory.' What was the effect of a view of God on his mind? 'Wo is me!' said Isaiah; 'wo is me! for I am undone, because I am a man of unclean lips, and I dwell in the midst of a people of unclean lips; for mine eyes have seen the King, the Lord of Hosts!" *Hear that man saying that he is perfect, that he is pure from his sins. Is he? I ask again—is he? I doubt that man.* [Mr. F., we hope, will pardon others, if they continue to "doubt that man."] What! when Isaiah had but a glimpse of God and of heaven, it was so holy that he was overwhelmed. he could not endure it, his self-abasement was so great that until an angel took a live coal from off the altar, and touched his lips and assured him his sins were forgiven, he was in despair. *This is the natural result of having a clear view of God.* It makes a person sink down in self-abasement lower and *lower* and LOWER, so that when he comes into the presence of God, he wants to find a place so infinitely low before God, words cannot express it."

This was Charles G. Finney the revival preacher and the lecturer on revivals; and these were his sentiments in the days of his greatest physical, and intellectual vigor, and when, in the estimation even of his present admirers, his labors were the most blessed in the conversion of souls. How absurd then to argue that his present views—standing in such striking and mournful contrast with those which he then held—must be correct because his labors were in those days so much blessed in revivals! The argument really amounts to this: God greatly blessed Mr. Finney's preaching in those revivals; therefore the sentiments which he then held and proclaimed, are false, and those which, in the days of his greatest power, he regarded with so much abhorrence are true and excellent! To impute Mr. Finney's former usefulness to his present theory of sinless perfection, is a very arbitrary species of imputation certainly. It would be well for the advocates of this theory to inquire whether Mr. F's success in saving souls has been *greater* since his change of views than before. And we would recommend that the same inquiry be extended, with proper diligence and accuracy, to the case of Mr. Mahan and any others of kindred views.* Has their success in revivals of religion been *increased* in consequence of their change of sentiment? If effort, blessed to the salvation of souls, is to be taken as a test of correctness in doctrine, we would refer not only to the prosperous career of Luther, Knox, Baxter, Edwards, Whitefield, Brainerd, Davies, Dwight, Payson, Griffin, Beecher,

---

* It is worthy of remark, that Mr. Mahan, from his own showing, (see his Book, pp. 231, 232,) made his great attainments in holiness *precious* to his adoption of his present theory. It was after his desiring to be entirely consecrated—his exclamation, "I have found it"—and his discovery that he ought to go to Christ for sanctification, as well as justification—that some one proposed, in a meeting, this question: "When we look to Christ for sanctification, what degree of sanctification may we expect from him? May we look to him to be sanctified wholly, or not?" Mr. M. says: "I do not know that I was ever so shocked or confounded before or since. I felt, for the moment, that the work of Christ among us would be marred, and the mass of minds around us rush into Perfectionism." That is, even then, the question, "may we look to Christ to be sanctified wholly?" shocked and awfully confounded him. Did he then *expect* that himself, or others, would be sanctified in this life *wholly?* Yet, when this admission had been pointed out as bearing against his theory of *expectation*, he came out in the B b. Repos. (of Oct. 1840, p. 423) and declared that he was *practically* under the influence of the sentiment which *theoretically* so shocked and confounded him. Says he: "The redemption of Christ was *then* presented to my mind as a *full* and *perfect* redemption. I *felt* that in Christ I was 'complete'—that in him *every demand of my being was met.* In this light I presented him to others." We would not intimate that Mr. M's sketch of his experience, is in any respect a fancy picture; or that he did not feel all the horror he expressed in relation to that "question;" or that he was not under the wholesome "*practical*" influence of an expectation, or a sentiment, the very suggestion of which was, "*theoretically*," "shocking" and "confounding" to him, even some time *after* it had wrought its "perfect work." But we think all this must have been according to some principle in mental philosophy not long since discovered; or at least that his "recognition of the states of his own mind" must have been too imperfect to qualify him "to testify to his own entire sanctification."

Beman, Kirk, and all the other *most successful* revival preachers of the day, but to the former success of Mr. Finney and Mr.
Mahan themselves, as at least a fair off-set to whatever of saving
power may have attended their labors, since the adoption of their
present theory of sanctification.* We speak advisedly when we
say that some of the warmest friends of Mr. Finney, as he *was*,
regret his change of views, mainly on account of the disastrous
influence of this change upon the spirit of revivals. These remarks relating to Mr. F. we thought due to the cause of truth.
We have no inducement to speak disparagingly of his former
successful efforts to win souls to Christ; but we do protest against
their being considered as the fruit of those branches on his theological tree which have been engrafted, or have budded and
grown since since the year 1835, in place of those which flour-
ished upon it in the days of his revivals. Nor are we disposed
to overlook or underrate whatever there may be of good spirit
or of good intention at Oberlin. Yet, as the result of much ob-
servation, as well as of careful inquiry, (through the friends
quite' as much as through the opposers of Oberlin,) during the
last five years, it is our most decided conviction, that whatever
of truly benevolent spirit—of humilty—or of zeal for the conversion of souls, may exist in the institution, remains there not in
consequence, but in spite of their theory of sinless perfection.
The conceit of possessing extraordinary light in the things of
religion, with contempt for the opinions and usages of others, a
spirit of self-exaggeration extending itself to whatever apper-
tains to the success of their views, and an unresisted temptation
to cherish a less elevated and spiritual idea of the Law of God,
have evidently marked the introduction, progress and development of their perfectionism.† While there has been much said

---

* The *decline* of interest in the conversion of souls, among the Professors
and students at Oberlin, within the last year or two—and especially among
those claiming to be entirely sanctified—has been so apparent in their prayers and other religious exercises, as to have been a subject of frequent remark
with intelligent observers who have spent much time there, and has been
sometimes acknowledged even by the friends of that institution. A mother
in Israel—who has ever been a steadfast friend to the institution, and was
fully possessed of the facts in the case—said nearly a year ago, (without intending to give the remark any bearing on the theory in question.) "Oberlin
is not what it used to be. Formerly sinners were converted there. But now
the attention of Christians is so much absorbed in other things, that sinners
are neglected, un' become hardened." The Rev. Mr. ——, an ardent and
well known friend of Oberlin, and also of the theory of sinless perfection,
speaking of a protracted meeting held by Mr. ——, who has been understood
to consider himself in a state of entire sanctification, said (incidentally) nearly
two years ago, "There were not many conversions. *The truth is, of late,
Brother ——'s preaching is not well fitted to convict sinners. It is better adapted
for Heaven than for this world."* This was evidently intended for praise, and
not for censure.

† "The Lynching case at Oberlin," illustrates this remark. That transaction doubtless originated in a state of feeling such as we have described.

(no doubt honestly) about a "higher standard of religion," the
actual tendency of things has been to lower the standard.

The system tends, (as we have seen,)

1. *To lower down the demands of God's law.* Consequently,

2. *To foster spiritual pride.* As Mr. Finney once remarked: "If a person compares himself with a low standard, he will
think he is doing pretty well." Of course, then,

3. *To cherish egotism, self-ignorance, and carnal security.*
This will be increased by the habit of regarding the notices of
consciousness as sufficiently full and accurate to enable one to
testify to his own entire sinlessness. Also,

The writing of the amatory letters to the young man, "involving falsehood,
forgery and hypocrisy;" the continuing to justify this, virtually, on the principle that "the end sanctifies the means;" and by taking, not the Law of God,
but the practice of "police magistrates and post office agents," as their
standard of action—the *deliberate* manner in which they made up their minds
how to punish the individual so craftily detected—whether by "tarring and
feathering," by "ducking," or by "whipping"—the "*engaging in a season of
prayer,*" for direction as to the best mode of committing lawless violence—
the going and taking advice of a Theological Professor, who said, "If you
catch him, give him a good flogging, and send him out of town," or possibly,
"treat him roughly"—having "in his mind at the time (by some unaccounta-
ble association of ideas) the manner in which Gideon taught the men of Suc-
coth" (see Judges 8: 7—16)—the gagging, blindfolding, and whipping, to the
amount of between twenty and thirty lashes, inflicted upon "the bare back"
of one who had been committed by a pious father to the care of the Faculty,
and should have been admonished by them with paternal faithfulness, and if
incorrigible, expelled lawfully from the institution—all this, on the common
plea made in every instance of Lynching, viz. its being a case for which the
civil law did not provide—or, "the moral purity of Oberlin required that they
should pursue such a course, in a case which the civil law did not reach;"
and by those, too, who, as Abolitionists, had often and justly condemned this
plea for mobs and lawless violence—can be viewed as nothing less than a
strongly marked example of fanaticism—fanaticism involving a ludicrously
exaggerated notion of the moral light which they possess, and the spiritual
attainments which they have made at Oberlin—(reminding not a few of Job
12: 2)—and of the transcendent importance of that Institution to the success
and even to the existence of vital piety in the world—(making whatever
relates to its prosperity so momentous as to justify a disregard of the civil
law)—and an attachment to a theory which, while it fosters this notion,
tends to produce less elevated and spiritual views of God's Law. For the
facts in "the Lynching case," see the Ohio Observer of Dec. 24; the New
York Observer of Jan. 9, and Feb. 6; and the New York Evangelist of Jan.
30. The more this affair is looked into, the worse it appears, and we doubt
whether all of the more discreditable features of the transaction are yet fully
known to the public. But the profound silence, for more than six months,
of the Faculty of Oberlin, touching this affair, in which one or more of their
own number were concerned, (as well as many of the students,) and of the
Oberlin Evangelist, too, though its editor figured largely in the outrage—the
attempt, on the part of most of the advocates of "Oberlin Perfectionism"
there and elsewhere, to pass over the whole matter as "*nothing,*" or to apol-
ogize for it on various and contradictory grounds—and the justification of
"*the correspondence,*" "the gagging," "blindfolding," and all, except perhaps
"the whipping"—may, we think, be regarded as being quite as lucid a commentary upon the tendencies of the Oberlin system, as "the Lynching case"
itself.

4. *To foster contempt of pastoral instruction, advice, and admonition.* One who fancies that he has received "the New Covenant," and is now illuminated and guided by "an indwelling Christ"—"the author of all his feelings and actions"—will not (though Messrs. Finney and Mahan should strongly protest against this legitimate and natural result of such principles) be apt to give much heed to the teachings of fallible men. And,

5. *To produce neglect of the ordinances of the gospel.* Will a person who believes that he is thus illuminated—inhabited—and guided by "the Eternal Life of the soul," be likely to realize his need of outward forms and symbols, to bring to *his* mind "the things of Christ?"

6. *To the disuse of prayer for the sanctifying influences of the Spirit.* A sense of need is the basis of such prayer. But one who thinks he is entirely purified already, and that his cup is full to running over, is more likely to imitate the spirit of the prayer recorded in Luke 18: 11, 12, than that in the 13th verse of the same chapter.

7. *To "Antinomian Perfectionism."* Some may ask what are the peculiarities of this sort of Perfectionism? We have given extracts from the writings of the Oberlin Professors, for a description of their own peculiar doctrines: we will permit one of their associates to exhibit the prominent features of "Antinomian Perfectionism." A writer in the Oberlin Evangelist, who is one of the Professors at Oberlin, has furnished an analysis of this system. presenting the following points:

"1. *It disclaims all obligation to obey the Moral Law.* It does this with a profession of substituting the law of love in its stead, overlooking the fact, that the Moral Law is God's own embodied and developed *law of love.* They therefore blindly reject God's Law of love and adopt their own.*

"2. The system supposes the Christian to receive Christ within him in such a way, that henceforth Christ only acts within him; and whatever himself seems to do, Christ really does. Some even suppose their own individual being to be absorbed or merged into Christ, so that themselves, as distinct persons, have ceased to exist, and all that was themselves is now Christ. This is the oriental doctrine revived, that man is a

---

* The leading writers among the Antinomian Perfectionists have continued to deny that they disclaim obligation to obey the Moral Law. And Mr. Finney (O. Evan. vol. 2, p. 49) says: "With respect to the modern Perfectionists, those who have been acquainted with their writings, *know that some of them have gone much farther from the truth than others. Some of their leading men,* who commenced with them, and adopted their name, stopped far short of adopting some of their most abominable errors: still maintaining the authority and perpetual obligation of the Moral Law; and thus have been saved from going into many of the most objectionable and destructive notions of that sect." That is, they have stopped far short of adopting the legitimate conclusions to be drawn from their own premises.

spark emanating from the Deity, which ultimately returns, and is swallowed up again in the Divine Essence.*

"Hence 3. The system, either avowedly or virtually, annihilates personal agency and responsibility. In the language of one: "On the — day of ——, I received Christ as a whole Saviour. I died, and in my expiring breath, bequeathed my body, soul and spirit to the Lord, and cast the responsibility upon him, of keeping me forever from all sin †

"4. As a consequence, mental impressions, *supposed* to be from the Spirit of God, are deemed perfect truth and law, paramount even to the Bible itself. Some are prophets in the higher sense, enjoying a very peculiar union with Christ, and their word is far above the Bible.‡

"5. These principles lead more or less extensively, as the case may be, to the rejection of all gospel ordinances, the disuse of prayer, and all manner of licentiousness. This is not given as a *universal* result: but an occasional one; or rather, it may be said, a *legitimate* one, to which the system inherently tends, and which it speedily reaches, unless there be some happy inconsistency between the principles and the practice." §

These are all the points which the writer specifies; and it should be borne in mind, that he was far more anxious to make

---

* Compare this with the following sentiments of Mr. Finney (O. Evan. vol. 1, p. 10): Faith "is that opening of the door of the heart spoken of in the scripture, and receiving Christ as an indwelling and reigning King."— "Hence he is represented as *dwelling in us—which I suppose to be really and literally true*—that by his Spirit he is *personally* present with the mind, and by his truth and persuasive influences *controlling, guiding* and *directing it.*"— "*He is the life or the holiness of the soul.* It is his presence and agency that produces holiness in us; and this holiness continues no longer and extends no farther than the Divine agency that produces it."—"*Christ is the perpetual author of all our holy feelings and actions.*"—Mr. F., we ought to say, carefully protests against certain natural inferences from these premises. But we ask: is the Perfection st sentiment given above, anything more than an *ultraism*, or a farther carrying out of Mr. F's own speculations?

† Compare this with the following from Mr. Mahan's Book, p. 110. Speaking of the conditions of receiving the New Covenant, he mentions that, "An actual reception of Christ, and reliance upon him for all those blessings, in all their fulness—*a surrender of your whole being to him*, that he may accomplish in you all the "exceeding great and precious promises" of the New Covenant. When this is done: when there is that full and implicit reliance upon Christ, for the entire fulfilment of all that he has promised, *he becomes directly responsible for our full and complete redemption.*"—"*To us his word stands pledged*," "*to give us one heart and one way, that we may fear God forever*"—"*finally, to sanctify us wholly and preserve our whole spirit and soul and body blameless unto the coming of our Lord Jesus Chr st.*" If this be not identical with the sentiment above, there is surely resemblance enough to justify a claim of relationship.

‡ It must be obvious that *like* principles, in the two systems, must tend to *like* results. That this theoretical tendency of the Oberlin system has been attended with *no* corresponding results, we should hardly dare even now to affirm, although its entire development has by no means, as yet, been reached.

§ The same remark is applicable to this point as to the preceding.

out a *contrast*, than a *resemblance*, between that system and his own. The Professor then proceeds:

"We pass to the causes which have led to this system.

"1. A strong conviction that the Church *is utterly wrong*, and that themselves have been wrong too, and of course that *something else must be tried;*—their views being commonly vague, as to what the *wrong thing is*, or *the right thing* either, and their *feelings* being usually *ardent*, and their *impulses strong*.*

"2. Some have toiled in a legal religion, until, sick with such efforts, they rush into the opposite extreme. From trying to do everything without Christ, the transition is not unnatural to making Christ do everything.†

"3. *Spiritual pride*. Of this, the extreme and bitter censoriousness, said to be common among them, is sufficient proof. The fact, if such it be, accounts adequately for God's leaving them to so strange a delusion.‡

---

* How deeply the authors of Oberlin Perfectionism have sympathized with their brethren of the other system, in relation to what is here mentioned, their writings abundantly show. The *fact*, that the *practice* of the Church is in no small degree inconsistent with the *principles* wh ch they profess, and which their consciences approve, and their hearts in some degree love, is so very obvious that it requires no great degree of spiritua discernment to per--ceive it, and make it a topic of denunciation. And the absurd inference, that the *principles which they fail to live up to, must be wrong*, and that *"of course something else must be tried,"* has been drawn by too many infidels and heresiarchs, as well as inconsiderate Christians, to excite admiration by its novelty. Several somewhat popular systems of spurious Christianity and false philosophy now before the public, are virtually advocated with the following argument:—"1. There is a great deal of worldiness, and other inconsistency in the Church. 2. Therefore the prevailing doctrines, and the mode of teaching them adopted by ministers, are rad cally false, and ought to be discarded. 3. And therefore the system to which Heaven has at last directed our inquiring minds, is the one which the Church needs, and must adopt before the Millennium can be introduced."—Were the *doctrines* false, or badly taught, which Paul proclaimed, because the Corinthians became contentious and disorderly, and the Galatians proved unstable, and the Ephesians fell from their first love?—The sort of reformation now most needed, is not the marking out of *new ways*—nor the invention of *new theories*, to be *"tried"* as experiments in the Church of God, but *better walking in "the old paths"*—more *faithful living up to principles long acknowledged*.

† That there has heretofore been a strong disposition among the great mass of those who now favor Oberlin Perfectionism, to rely upon their own resolutions, and to overlook their need of Divine grace to work in them both to will and to do, has been observed and lamented, by some of the most judicious Christians in this country; and their rapid transition to the opposite extreme, at the present time, is equally notorious and lamentable.

‡ How far the authors of Oberlin Perfectionism differ from them, in this particular, may be seen abundantly in their writings. As a mere specimen, we give the following from the O. Evan. vol. 2, p. 28. Mr. Finney asks. "Are not the Church, in their present state, a standing, public, perpetual denial of the gospel? Do they not stand out before the world as a living unanswerable contradiction of the gospel: and do more to harden sinners. and lead them into a spirit of caviling and infidelity, than all the efforts of professed infidels, from the beginning of the world to the present day?" and these, with a long list of other and similar charges, occupying more than two columns of the O. Evan., are said to be but a "hint at the facts as they

"4. A literal construction of certain highly figurative, or rather peculiarly metaphysical expressions in the Bible. 'I live, yet not I, but Christ liveth in me,' is an instance.*

"5. A natural tendency in enthusiastic minds to regard themselves as the special favorites of Heaven, and perfectly inspired both with knowledge of truth and impulse in duty.

"6. It is presumed that most of the leading minds which have gone into this delusion, have been somewhat distinguished for one or both of these two qualities, viz. *self conceit* and *instability.*" (See O. Evan. vol. 1, p. 22.)†

Such, then, are the prominent features and causes of "Antinomian Perfectionism." Had the Oberlin system been "sitting for the picture," we see not what more would have been requisite than a little more *age*—a little more *growth* of two or three of its features—to make it "a likeness," under which it would have been needless to write the name.‡ Although the Oberlin Professors may as honestly abhor certain conclusions, as did the leaders of the Antinomian Perfectionists, and may, like them, stop far short of some of the worst of those conclusions, yet we can discover, neither in their theory of sinless perfection, nor in the doctrines associated with it, any conservative principle, or counteracting tendency, to prevent it from running downward in the

---

exist almost every where." The Synod of Genessee very justly remark: "We deem this a most gross slander of the Church of Christ. At no period of the world has the Church done so much for the world's conversion as is now doing; and never have there been so great revivals, at home and among our missions, as in the present age: and the fruits borne by the whole Church, contradict most powerfully the slander above quoted." Mr. Finney's denunciatory communication, of which the above is a part, was published on the 12th of February last—at a time when, in nearly every section of our country. revivals of almost unprecedented power were gladdening the hearts of God's people.

* That the authors of the Oberlin system have but little *advantage* over them, in this respect, has been sufficiently shown.

† Whether the authors of Oberlin Perfectionism are unusually free from *enthusiastic* tendencies, or may justly be considered as possessed, in an extraordinary degree, of either of the two qualities, *self-diffidence* and *stability,* is a question on which it is both needless and improper for us to discuss.

‡ The Wesleyan doctrine of "Christian Perfection" is not only different in itself from the Oberlin theory, but held in connection with different views of native depravity—of the heart—of moral agency—of the nature of sanctification, etc. Mr. Wesley's perfect Christian, is one who nevertheless does that which, "were it not for the blood of atonement, would expose to eternal damnation." "The most perfect," according to him, "have continual need of the merits of Christ, even for their actual transgressions, and may say for themselves, as well as for their brethren. 'Forgive us our trespasses.'" That is, his is a sort of "imperfect perfection." He objects to calling it "sinless perfection." Those Methodists who have been at the pains to analyze the Oberlin system, regard it as differing very widely from their own. A writer in "the Christian Advocate and Journal," of June 19. after making various strictures upon the Oberlin theory, says: "It is not the Arminian theory. It is Pelagian Perfectionism, and the truth will suffer loss, if we permit the public to be misled by the supposition that their theory and ours are the same."

direction of the worst form of Antinomianism. It seems to us morally certain, that many, very many of those who embrace the system, will be carried along in the strong current of its tendencies, though some of its authors or advocates may not be swept down so far as others. The reflecting reader must have observed that there is in the system a peculiar combination of doctrines, all tending directly or indirectly the same way; and that the arguments in its behalf all prove too much if they prove anything—that they generally include, within their bearing, some of the worst positions of the Antinomian Perfectionists. The system evidently is not yet fully developed. Several causes have held its natural tendencies in check. Under the influence of habits acquired through a better theory, and with no small anxiety for the credit of their principles, and having before their eyes the scandal of a system earlier developed, to warn them, its advocates may not *at once* run into *some* of the practices into which certain other Perfectionists have gone; such as the disuse of the ordinances of the gospel, and of religious ceremonies. With their solicitude to avoid even the appearance of these things, and under the influence of their doctrine of *dietetic* or *physiological depravity*, not a few of them perhaps will run into the other extreme, and make religion to consist mainly in things outward, especially in "physiological habits."

In view of the whole subject we would say:

1. That if it is through the *truth* that God sanctifies his people, Oberlin Perfectionism can only hinder the work of grace in their hearts.

2. That any who suppose they have been benefitted by reading the Oberlin Evangelist, and other works devoted to the propagation of this system of error, are probably deceived in one of two ways: either they are mistaken in thinking they are growing in grace, or they have been benefitted by what constitutes no part of the *peculiarities* of that system; and would have been far more benefitted, and less injured, if they had devoted the same amount of time to the practical writings of such men as Flavel, Owen, Baxter, Bunyan, Doddridge, Scott, Henry and Nevins.

3. That the facility with which not a few, who once abhorred Wesleyan Perfectionism, have been led to embrace a theory far more extravagant and pernicious, should be set down among the darker signs of the times, and as indicating the importance of more thorough and discriminating doctrinal instruction in the churches, as well as of a deeper reverence for the teachings of God's word, and less regard for the opinions of men.

S. B. CANFIELD
S. C. AIKEN. } *Com. of Presbytery.*
H. BLODGET.

ERRATA.—On 4th page, 2d line from top, for *doctrines* read *doctrines;* 35th p. 9th line from bottom, for *relate* read *relates;* 53d page, in note, bottom line, insert *every other* before *sin,* and in the 2d line insert *other* before *sin.*